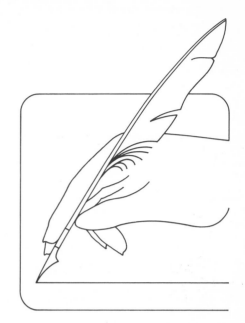

WORLD OF CULTURE

POETRY

by J.D. O'Hara

Newsweek Books, New York

NEWSWEEK BOOKS

Joseph L. Gardner, Editor

Janet Czarnetzki, Art Director
Edwin D. Bayrd, Jr., Associate Editor
Frances J. Owles, Copy Editor
Ellen Kavier, Writer-Researcher
Susan Storer Gombocz, Picture Researcher   ARNOLDO MONDADORI EDITORE

S. Arthur Dembner, President   Mariella De Battisti, Picture Researcher
Alvin Garfin, Publisher   Giovanni Adamoli, Production Coordinator

Frontispiece: George Gordon, Lord Byron memorabilia

Contents

1

The Language of the Imagination

As keepers of their culture's oral history, poets enjoyed particularly exalted status in ancient times. So did poetry itself, which was considered the special province of priests and philosophers, sovereigns and seers. It is altogether logical, then, that the Sufis, a Moslem mystic order, should have produced Persia's greatest poets, among them Hafiz, Jami, and Omar Khayyám. Shown opposite is a finely detailed miniature of a Persian poet in his garden.

DESPITE WHAT SOME PEOPLE SAY, the oldest profession may actually be that of poet. Whales chant and sing; apes and chimpanzees beat the ground and hoot and holler rhythmically; and even the most primitive of human tribes preceded their hunting expeditions, feasts, and funerals with organized and rhythmic boasting, cheering, or lamentation. Storytellers found long ago that stories were more easily memorized when they were worded rhythmically, and that audiences delighted in the repetition of familiar terms and phrases: "the wine-surfaced sea," "rosy-fingered dawn," "once upon a time, and a very good time it was." Early narratives are full of formulas like these, which modern readers may find irritating but which listeners still enjoy—and which constitute another form of rhythmic repetition.

What is true of mankind's childhood is also true of individual children: they like to chant and sing, to exaggerate the accents of words and sentences, to repeat the same sounds and phrases. They even develop little tunes and pass them on from generation to generation; in America these include such skip-rope chants as "A, my name is Alice" and such mocking shouts as "Johnny is a sissy" and "I know what you're doing."

We like to play with language, to repeat sounds for their own sake, as in "ho-hum," "fiddle-faddle," and "tra-la-la." When we can do so and make sense, we like it even more. And when we can make sense imaginatively instead of literally, our enjoyment is even greater. One way in which we make sense is to make connections among things: John is Jim's brother; dogs and cats are animals. But the most amusing kinds of connections are imaginative and metaphorical rather than literal. When we say that a man is in the autumn of his life, for instance, we make a connection that is farfetched, not rational, and our minds have to stretch a little to encompass the idea. If the connection is also phrased interestingly, using rhythm and sounds, then we like it even more, as when Macbeth says, "my way of life is fall'n into the sear, the yellow leaf," or when Shakespeare develops this same idea further:

> That time of year thou mayst in me behold
> When yellow leaves, or none, or few, do hang
> Upon those boughs which shake against the cold,
> Bare ruin'd choirs, where late the sweet birds sang. . . .

Shakespeare makes more connections among sounds, images, and ideas than most people ever manage by themselves, but essentially he does precisely what we all do when we say "dead as a doornail," "free as a bee," or "snug as a bug in a rug."

Some connections are very farfetched indeed. Homer's "rosy-fingered dawn" turns dawn into a woman. Hamlet's

> But look, the morn in russet mantle clad
> Walks o'er the dew of yon high eastward hill

carries the connection even further; and Samuel Butler's comparison achieves a delightful absurdity:

> Now, like a lobster boil'd, the morn
> From black to red begins to turn.

But the three-year-old who calls a visitor "corn on the cob" and the adult who refers to an enemy as a "snake in the grass" are doing the same sort of thing, both of them enjoying improbable connections, repeated sounds, and even the same little rhythmic tune. We are all poets—or at least we are all poetic.

Poetry also deals in other kinds of connection. Brooding over his father and stepfather, Hamlet connects them with images of extreme virtue and sensual evil:

> So excellent a king, that was to this
> Hyperion to a satyr.

Alexander Pope, summing up man's paradoxical position between Hyperion and a satyr, makes more complicated connections, locating us within a cluster of opposing qualities:

> Know then thyself, presume not God to scan;
> The proper study of Mankind is Man.
> Placed on this isthmus of a middle state,
> A Being darkly wise, and rudely great:
> With too much knowledge for the Sceptic side,
> With too much weakness for the Stoic's pride,
> He hangs between; in doubt to act, or rest,
> In doubt to deem himself a God, or Beast;
> In doubt his Mind or Body to prefer,
> Born but to die, and reasoning but to err;
> Alike in ignorance, his reason such,
> Whether he thinks too little, or too much:
> Chaos of Thought and Passion, all confused;
> Still by himself abused, or disabused;
> Created half to rise, and half to fall;
> Great lord of all things, yet a prey to all;
> Sole judge of Truth, in endless Error hurled:
> The glory, jest, and riddle of the world!

We connect parts of the world whenever we express them together, even if we do so in order to emphasize differences or discrepancies. With its compactness, its freedom to range through time and space in search of images, and its ability to hold things together not only with grammar but with sounds and rhythms, poetry has always been wonderfully equipped to connect parts of the world and to connect us to the world.

> Ah, Sunflower! weary of time,
> Who countest the steps of the Sun,
> Seeking after that sweet golden clime
> Where the traveller's journey is done. . . .

So William Blake begins a poem . . . and so the weary heliotropic flower is connected both with the sun on its continuous circular journey around the earth and with a human traveler on his own journey, heaven and nature and mankind sharing a common burden of time, and feeling a common longing for eternity and rest. It is a remarkable feat of connection, though less ambitious than those connections Blake imagines when he urges us

> To see a world in a grain of sand
> And a heaven in a wild flower,
> Hold infinity in the palm of your hand
> And eternity in an hour.

Poetry also calls our attention to the connections in language, as we have seen. It repeats sounds, it organizes and intensifies accents, and it repeats words and ideas just as we do when talking excitedly. In the biblical book of Judges, when Deborah and Barak sing about Jael's killing of the dreaded enemy leader Sisera, they dwell on the event as if they cannot stop talking about it:

> She put her hand to the nail, and her right hand to the
> workman's hammer;
> and with the hammer she smote Sisera,
> she smote off his head,
> when she had pierced and stricken through his temples.
> At her feet he bowed, he fell, he lay down:
> at her feet he bowed, he fell:
> where he bowed, there he fell down dead.

The Hebrew poet has expressed excitement by repeating his ideas and phrasing while varying his rhythms and sounds, but a similar kind of excitement can be evoked in other ways. The English poet Swinburne, for instance, typically uses a rush of imagery expressed in quick rhythms and in long sentences that are at once tied together and hurried on by repeated alliterations and rhymes. Few people have claimed fully to understand such verses as the following, but most agree that they sound very exciting:

> When the hounds of spring are on winter's traces,
> The mother of months in meadow or plain
> Fills the shadows and windy places
> With lisp of leaves and ripple of rain;
> And the brown bright nightingale amorous
> Is half assuaged for Itylus,

During Japan's imperial epoch verse-making was an integral part of court life. A noble's standing among his peers could rise dramatically or fall precipitately on the basis of a single extemporaneous poem—and a courtier's calligraphic style was considered an index of his character. At left is a sumi-e *ink drawing of the poet Sosei Hoshi; below, a scroll detail that combines portraits of two court poets with calligraphed examples of their verse.*

9

For the Thracian ships and the foreign faces,
The tongueless vigil, and all the pain.

Drab as they may sound in themselves, repetition and connection are primary causes of excitement; and excitement is one of the great aims of poetry. This stimulation need not be emotional or sensual, as we have seen. When Pope asks us to recognize mankind's strange position in the world—or when Blake asks us to connect the general with the particular and extremes with their opposites—both poets are appealing especially to our capacity for intellectual excitement, although both give an emotional tone to what they say, as everyone who takes ideas seriously must do.

Repetition and connection enable poets to increase the intensity of what they say. Paradoxically, they also give poets—and the rest of us—more control over language and emotion, and therefore more control over expression. We have all felt highly wrought up at various times in our lives: after a good movie or a rock concert, after receiving a piece of wonderful news or watching a dazzling touchdown run, after participating in intense conversation or passionate lovemaking. At such times we feel the need to let off steam and express our feelings—and not merely by jumping up and down, waving our arms, and shouting words at random. We want to focus our intensity, to give it form. What results is not random shouts but a cheer, not mere jumping but a dance, not howls but a song. And in literature, repetition and connection are the chief elements that shape and order and organize the author's thoughts and feelings in such a way as to lead his readers by stages through a patterned as well as intense experience.

Naturally enough, the poet often uses the patterns employed by the prose writer—plot and chronology. But while the prose writer generally confines himself to sentences, paragraphs, and chapters, the poet uses many other intricate arrangements of sound and sense, always with the object of connecting and intensifying his material. For Samuel Taylor Coleridge, this ability was the chief glory of poetic power. "This power," he wrote, "reveals itself in the balance or reconciliation of opposite or discordant qualities: of sameness, with difference; of the general, with the concrete; the idea, with the image; the individual, with the representative; the sense of novelty and freshness, with old and familiar objects; a more than usual state of emotion, with more than usual order; judgment ever awake and steady self-possession, with enthusiasm and feeling profound or vehement; and while it blends and harmonizes the natural and the artificial, still subordinates art to nature; the manner to the matter; and our admiration of the poet to our sympathy with the poetry."

There are many kinds of excitement and many ways to arouse it and shape it through language. Mankind has spent thousands of years exploring the resources of language without exhausting them. These explorations have developed and accentuated the best features that language has to offer, and poets have gradually accumulated standard methods of procedure, standard forms of poetry, and conventional subject matter. During this long process the art of poetry has become

The cult of the poet reached its apogee in Japan during the brief lifetime of Matsuo Basho, popularizer of the epigrammatic verse form known as haiku. Basho was only thirty at the time of his death in 1694, but he was already acknowledged as the unrivaled master of his nation's unique fixed-syllable poetic forms. The contemporary screen painting opposite, attributed to Tatebayashi Kagei and entitled Thirty-six Immortal Poets, *features a gathering of Basho's illustrious predecessors.*

10

highly sophisticated and specialized, at times so specialized as to put it out of the reach of the ordinary human.

Other kinds of specialization, more common and more valuable, arise from a culture's inherited patterns of thought and expression and from the nature of its language. The Japanese language, for instance, is almost without stress; it would therefore be difficult to use it for the composition of metrical verse. On the other hand, since all Japanese syllables are approximately the same length, the Japanese can "hear" syllable counts. Several of their most popular poetic forms, therefore, are composed of lines containing a fixed number of syllables. A *haiku* is made up of three lines of five, seven, and five syllables; a *tanka* has five lines of five, seven, five, seven, and seven syllables. These brief forms are popular in part because Japanese culture has traditionally urged a

11

The predictable pattern of haiku verse, which usually evokes a particular season, mood, and subject, has a natural ally in the Japanese wood-block print, which easily encompasses the same essential elements. This delicately colored print, executed in 1835 by master printmaker Ando Hiroshige, illustrates the poem:

> Autumn of dreams,
> Looking cry begins
> Summer quail.

concentration of vision and thought upon those small events and scenes that condense large issues. One form of *haiku*, for instance, obliges the writer within his seventeen syllables to evoke a season of the year, a time of day, and a mood.

Japanese poets are by no means the lone practitioners of such fixed-syllable versemaking. Chinese poets, whose written language bears a superficial resemblance to Japanese and whose spoken tongue is vastly different, also use syllabic verse, to which they often add rhyme and regulated tonal patterns. Traditional Welsh poetry is also syllabic, with exhausting patterns of rhyme and slant rhyme. In classical Greek poetry, the verses are composed in arrangements of long and short syllables. And even though Latin, like English, is an accentual language, the early Roman poets imitated Greek prosody, so that Latin poetry and Latin colloquial speech sounded quite different from one other.

The same kind of arbitrary specialization took place in Irish poetry, not only in the verse forms but in the language, the rhetorical patterns, and the modes of thought. Irish poets were held in extremely high esteem—even after King Conchubar revoked the law by which only poets could be judges. (What good was it to have such learned men discussing cases, he argued, when the king himself could understand only half of what they said?) Even the apparently simple convention of rhyme varies with the culture using it. English rhyme begins with the last stressed vowel and consonant (carrying, parrying); the French delight in identical rhymes (*l'amour, la mort*); Arabic verse rhymes on the final consonants alone, and so on.

The complications of prosody are of little interest to non-speakers of a language—except to remind us as we read English verse that such respectable and solemn characteristics as rhyme, the iambic pentameter line hallowed by Shakespeare, Milton, Pope, and Wordsworth, and even the formal diction of traditional verse are not "natural" or "proper" but merely conventional and artificial; and what brings tears to an American reader's eye might make an African wince or smile.

Poets know that the conventions of verse are merely conventional, of course, and they often experiment with odd devices, hoping to find new ways of expanding the capabilities of language. They devise forms that exploit the possibilities of rhyme, such as the limerick, and they intensify grammatical repetitions. The eccentric eighteenth-century poet Christopher Smart once wrote a seventy-three-line poem about his cat in which each line begins with the word *for*, for instance. Smart's structure works, but it is good for that poem only; more commonly, poets contrive and pass on to their fellow artists forms that serve for many purposes. The sonnet is probably the best known of these, but there are many others with even more intense repetitions and connections. Their effect is suggested by Robert Bridges' triolet:

> When first we met we did not guess
> That Love would prove so hard a master;
> Of more than common friendliness
> When first we met we did not guess.
> Who could foretell this sore distress,
> This irretrievable disaster

> When first we met?—We did not guess
> That Love would prove so hard a master.

Verse has many patterns, line-lengths, syllable and stress qualities, and repetitions and combinations of sound and accent. In addition, some poets have taken advantage of the fact that verse is more often read than heard, and they have contrived visual patterns that give a poem a spatial as well as a verbal meaning. Some of these patterns are like the verbal structure of Smart's poem about his cat; poets have written poems about an ice cream cone, a building, a tree, that have the shape of their subject. Perhaps the best-known English poem of this sort appears in *Alice's Adventures in Wonderland* when Alice, listening dreamily to a mouse reciting a poem, discovers that the tale she hears and the tail she sees mingle with each other. More complicatedly, E. E. Cummings demonstrates the eye's difficulty in trying to focus on, keep up with, and finally identify a leaping grasshopper:

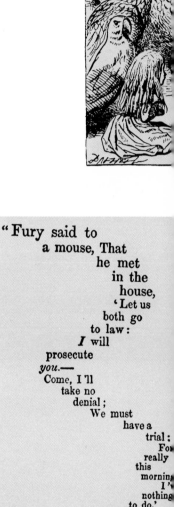

```
              r-p-o-p-h-e-s-s-a-g-r
                who
a)s w(e loo)k
upnowgath
             PPEGORHRASS
                             eringint(o-
aThe):1
            eA
                    !p:
S                                a
                     (r
rIvInG              .gRrEaPsPhOs)
                                     to
rea(be)rran(com)gi(e)ngly
,grasshopper;
```

It takes fifteen lines, a comic sonnet, for the grasshopper to finish leaping, get all its parts together, and "become rearrangingly" (or rearrange becomingly) into its identifiable self—although the semicolon ending tells us that it will not stay that way for long.

But the kinds of poetry that have meant the most to European and American readers down through the ages have had little to do with these complicated games of sounds and spaces. When we are interested in what poets can tell us about life and ourselves, we are likely to look for those larger forms of poetry that resemble such prose forms as the novel, the biography, the essay, even the sermon. Aside from the drama, the most popular form of poetry in the West has been the epic and its associated forms. Next in popularity are those forms that subordinate narrative to the author's comments: meditative poetry, visionary poetry, and satiric poetry, for instance. And, finally, there is the form now so popular as almost to eclipse the others—the lyric. None of these forms conforms to strict or even clear rules. Like the novel, which repeatedly eludes our definition, the epic, the meditation, the vision, even the lyric cannot be pinned down to fixed shapes, meters, and materials. This is no defect, except in the eyes of those scientists

```
   "Fury said to
       a mouse, That
          he met
             in the
                house,
            'Let us
              both go
             to law:
        I will
      prosecute
      you.—
      Come, I'll
         take no
           denial;
             We must
                 have a
                    trial:
                        For
                    really
                  this
                     morning
                       I'
                      nothing
                      to do.'
            Said the
             mouse to
           the cur,
             'Such a
                trial,
                dear sir,
            With no
         jury or
         judge,
          would be
            wasting
              our breath.'
               'I'll be
                 judge,
               I'll be
             jury,'
             Said
             cunning
              old Fury;
                'I'll try
                  the whole
                     cause,
                        and
                     condemn
                   you
                 to
                   death.'"
```

The first edition of Lewis Carroll's Alice's Adventures in Wonderland *was illustrated by the famed* Punch *illustrator and cartoonist Sir John Tenniel. Those celebrated engravings include the panel seen above, in which a rat declaims in verse before Alice and her companions. In the tired heroine's mind that poem assumes the shape of its teller's tail (left).*

Overleaf: The Mahabharata *is not only the longest epic poem in Sanskrit, it is the longest poem in any language—eight times as long as the* Iliad *and* Odyssey *combined. An eighteenth-century gouache painting depicts Krishna overcoming the serpent-demon Naga—one episode in this massive encyclopedia of Hindu life.*

who would like to categorize and label all the world. For most of us these loose forms encourage a corresponding openness of mind about the possibilities and varieties of literary expression.

The epic is one of the most impressive literary types ever developed. It tells an exciting story about a courageous and intelligent hero —and that in itself is enough to tax a poet's skills and to arouse great interest in his listeners. But added to these basic materials is a host of others: the epic hero is identifiably individual, but he is also the central public figure of a great historical event, the embodiment of important moral qualities, and a model for our admiration and imitation. His actions are watched by the gods, and the fate of a nation depends upon him. Coleridge told us that poetry unites the general with the concrete, the idea with the image, and the individual with the representative; not even the tragic drama does this better and on a grander scale than the epic. It is no wonder, then, that almost every culture developed forms of the epic early in its existence. In some cultures the epic provides a central storehouse for that society's beliefs, values, history, and ideals.

The earliest epics are quite literally compendiums of culture; often they have been put together out of many earlier, once separate stories, and often they have existed in many versions and forms before attaining their final shape. In fact some have never reached this kind of literary finality; the stories are still being joined, elaborated, and refined as they are retold down through the generations. Others have begun to disappear: the Babylonian epic *Gilgamesh*, which may be four thousand years old, is now only about half of what we imagine it to have been at one time, and this surviving half has been pieced together from almost 30,000 tablets and fragments in three different languages. Even in this partial form, however, *Gilgamesh* preserves many of the central features of the epic: it tells an exciting story, it focuses on a heroic warrior and ruler, and it takes its adventurous hero even into the world after death, a traditional location of superhuman wisdom.

Another early folk epic grew up on the other side of the Indus, in India, and grew to a truly epic size. The *Mahabharata*, a story of the descendants of the great king Bharata, probably came together as early as 500 B.C., although its present Sanskrit form was reached around A.D. 400. By far the longest poem ever composed—some 100,000 couplets— the *Mahabharata* tells the story of a protracted internecine struggle between the five sons of the dead King Pandu, called the Pandavas, and the hundred sons of Pandu's brother and successor, King Dhritarashtra. The Pandavas are the good guys; the sons of Dhritarashtra, especially Duryodhana, the eldest, are the bad guys; the variations and complications of their struggles are elaborated extensively, and the feud finally leads everyone to a climactic battle.

As they choose up sides, both the Pandavas and those allied with Duryodhana seek the services of Krishna, a relative of the Pandavas. He tells both sides that they can have the services of all his kinsmen or they can have him, but that he will take no active part in the fighting. Duryodhana chooses quantity, but one of the Pandavas, Arjuna, asks Krishna to be his charioteer. This is an inspired choice, for Krishna turns out to be an avatar of the god Vishnu. Arjuna and Krishna pre-

pare for the battle, and just before it begins they have a long conversation. This conversation, which is often read and studied separately, is the *Bhagavad-Gita*, the Song of Blessed God, a compilation and distillation of the central doctrines and beliefs of Hinduism and a primary source of Hindu influence on Western literature. American writers such as Thoreau and Emerson took its teachings to heart, and T. S. Eliot refers to the conversation between Krishna and Arjuna in his great religious poem *The Four Quartets*. As might be expected, the Pandavas win the battle, and after many more years and adventures the *Mahabharata* ends with the Pandavas achieving union with the godhead in eternity. Another ancient Indian epic, the *Ramayana*, tells of the many adventures that befall Prince Rama, another incarnation of Vishnu, and his wife, Sita. The *Ramayana* is only a quarter of the length of the *Mahabharata*—that is, only twice as long as the *Iliad* and the *Odyssey* combined.

Other Western cultures have approached the goal of a cumulative folk epic, but except in Greece those stories have remained separate, lacking a final, authoritative compiler and bard able to fuse them into one coherent whole. The *Mabinogion*, for instance, is a collection of eleven medieval Welsh tales, probably first told at least as early as the tenth century A.D., that provides early versions of many of the stories about the legendary King Arthur. And the *Poetic Edda*, assembled around A.D. 1000, contains thirty-four fragmentary poems by various authors, some of them about the Norse gods and others about the Volsungs—especially the noble, wise, and doomed Sigurd. Around A.D. 1200 this material was taken up again by an anonymous German poet. His *Nibelungenlied* is a long narrative about Siegfried (Sigurd) and his adventures with the dragon Fafnir and the Nibelung treasure, about the beautiful Brunhild and Siegfried's wife Kriemhild, and then about Siegfried's murder by an agent of his brother-in-law. In the second half of the poem Kriemhild marries Attila the Hun and sets out to get revenge on her brother—which she does, amid elaborate butchery. The story

India's other epic, the 24,000-stanza Ramayana, *details the exploits of Prince Rama, an incarnation of the Hindu god Vishnu. The bulk of the narrative concerns the young prince's attempts to rescue his wife, Sita, who is held captive by Ravana, the demon-king of Ceylon. Opposite: a cotton kerchief decorated with scenes from the* Ramayana. *The Teutonic equivalent of the legend of Rama is* The Nibelungenlied, *written in the late twelfth century by an anonymous German poet. The story itself is based upon a much earlier Scandinavian epic, the* Völsunga Saga, *whose hero is a prince named Sigurd. His life is the subject of the bas-reliefs seen at right.*

With the passage of time the legendary King Arthur—hero of England's early epic poem, the Mabinogion—has gradually subsumed the historical Arthur, a sixth-century Celtic knight. The manuscript illumination opposite shows King Arthur (top register) drawing the magical sword Excalibur from an anvil mounted on a large stone. Below, he lays the naked sword on an altar and receives his crown. The illustration at left, from the same thirteenth-century French manuscript, shows Arthur (left) riding into battle beneath the banner of his father, Uther Pendragon.

has often been retold, especially by Richard Wagner in his four-opera cycle *The Ring of the Nibelungs.*

One of the last of these folk collections apparently occurred in Scotland in the mid-eighteenth century when James Macpherson began to publish a series of poetic prose narratives that he described as translations from the early Gaelic poems of the bard Ossian. Their soggy melancholy and limp language have little in common with actual medieval writing, but the Ossianic poems were enormously popular with the sentimental readers of Macpherson's time and lent their falling rhythms to many a mournful writer. Macpherson was a fraud, of course. How far his "translations" strayed from epic toughness may be seen in this fragment from *Fingal: An Ancient Epic Poem* (1761):

> Weep on the rocks of roaring winds, O maid of Inistore! Bend thy fair head over the waves, thou lovelier than the ghost of the hills, when it moves in a sunbeam, at noon, over the silence of Morven! He is fallen! thy youth is low! pale beneath the sword of Cuthullin! No more shall valor raise thy love to match the blood of kings. Trenar, graceful Trenar died, O maid of Inistore! His bow is in the hall unstrung. No sound is in the hall of his hinds!

Far better as a deliberately composed folk epic is the Finnish *Kalevala,* which was put together by the Finnish writer and scholar Elias Lönnrot in the middle of the nineteenth century, using only the actual lines of traditional folk songs.

et lors aporta lespee toute nue en
tre ses mains si le menerent alau
tel et si le mit sus·

T quantil liot mise si le sacre
rent et enonissent et enfilleͬ
toutes iceles coses que ondoͤ

HPÆT PE GARDE
na ingear dagum· þeod cyninga
þrym ge frunon huða æþelingas elle̅
fre medon· oft scyld sceﬁng sceaþe
na þreatum monegū mægþum meodo setla
of teah egsode eorl syððan ærest peɼð
fea sceaft funden he þæs frofre geba
þeox under polcnum peorð myndum þah
oð þ him æghpylc þara ymb sitten dra
ofer hron rade hyran scolde zomban
gyldan þþæs god cyning· ðæm eafera pæs
æfter cenned geong ingeardum þone god
sende folce tofrofre fyren ðearfe on
geat þ hie ærdrugon aldo se lange
hpile him þæs liffrea puldres pealdend
porold are forgeaf beopulf pæs bren
blæd pide sprang scylde eafera scede
landum in· Spa sceal
ge pyrcean fromum feohgyftū on fæder

The Anglo-Saxon epic Beowulf, *composed by an unknown poet in the first decades of the eighth century, is the oldest extant written composition in English. Its highly complex construction, based on the repetition of consonants in stressed syllables —a common form of Old English verse—is revealed in surviving manuscript pages such as the one at far left. By the twelfth century, alliterative verse had been supplanted by the Continental rhyme schemes in which the* Song of Roland *and the* Poem of the Cid *were composed. At right is an illustration from the first printed edition of the latter. The* Kalevala, *Finland's national epic, existed only in oral form until the mid-1800s when philologist Elias Lönnrot compiled its 12,000 verses. At left, above, is a statue of Lemminkainen, one of the epic's three gallant heroes.*

There is also another kind of epic, one that derives from a close literary study of ancient models—especially the *Iliad* and the *Odyssey*—and that is created by one author. Vergil's *Aeneid* is the most famous of these, but there are numerous others. In England the eighth-century Anglo-Saxon author of *Beowulf* seems to have had the *Aeneid* in mind —as well as many Scandinavian and German models—when he composed his three-part poem in which the great hero and leader Beowulf tears an arm from the man-eating monster Grendel, then hunts down and kills Grendel's water-witch mother, and finally—in his old age— dies while saving his people from a fire-breathing dragon. Here, as in previous epics, there is a repeated insistence on the moral and spiritual implications of action; on proper and improper behavior; and on fate, courage, and the responsibility of a leader to his people. These topics recur frequently, but as the fragmentary plot suggests, the difficulties of the epic form clearly troubled the author of *Beowulf*, who found himself in a culture different in many ways from those early times when the epic sense of existence first developed.

Such difficulties led to lessenings of the epic, especially in the medieval *chanson de geste*, a verse narrative of military actions and heroic deeds represented by the Russian *Song of Igor's Campaign*, the French *Song of Roland*, and the Spanish *Poem of the Cid*—all written in the twelfth century. El Cid displays exemplary courage and chivalry during the battles between Christian Spain and Islam. Roland, the warrior companion of Oliver and an officer in Charlemagne's army fighting

the Saracens, also displays heroism, refusing to sound his horn and ask for aid from his emperor's central army until too late. Before he dies he realizes that his heroism has been vain and that Oliver's less pugnacious wisdom has had more value than he knew. Charlemagne's own view of life is still wider and deeper, partly because he gets advice from the angel Gabriel himself.

The sixteenth century saw a sudden surge in the popularity of the literary epic. Many were written and deservedly forgotten, but their very existence encouraged the composition of still better ones. In Italy two successful epic poets appeared, Ludovico Ariosto and Torquato Tasso. Both were well educated in classical literature, both were at home in elegant society, both served the noble Este family in Ferrara, and both wrote the new romantic kind of epic—highly self-conscious, stylized, episodic, witty, and focused as much on love as on heroism. Ariosto's *Orlando furioso*, completed in 1532, takes up a story begun by Matteo Boiardo some forty years earlier. In Boiardo's epic Roland falls in love with a pagan princess, rather oddly named Angelica, while the pagans are besieging Charlemagne in Paris. Ariosto then shows Roland as having gone mad for love. His wits are taken away— quite literally, to the moon—and he rages for three months. Then a sor-

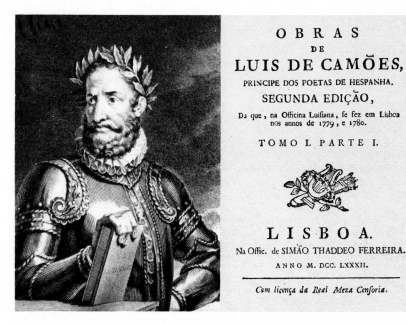

OBRAS
DE
LUIS DE CAMÕES,
PRINCIPE DOS POETAS DE HESPANHA.
SEGUNDA EDIÇÃO,
Da que , na Officina Luiſiana , ſe fez em Lisboa
nos annos de 1779 , e 1780.

TOMO I. PARTE I.

LISBOA.
Na Offic. de SIMÃO THADDEO FERREIRA.
ANNO M. DCC. LXXXII.

Com licença da Real Meza Cenſoria.

The sixteenth century witnessed the emergence of a new form of epic poetry, one that fused the national epic and the historical romance. These highly popular works, which emphasized amorous intrigue as well as high adventure, are epitomized by Ludovico Ariosto's Orlando furioso, *seen in an early edition below. Working in the study at left, Ariosto produced a fascinating sequel to the familiar tale of the paladin Roland. Luís vaz de Camões (near right), Ariosto's Portuguese contemporary, was himself an adventurer and had been blinded in one eye while battling the Moors. It was fitting, then, that he should compose* The Lusiads *(included in his collected works—title page, far right), a verse tribute to his nation's foremost naval hero, Vasco da Gama.*

ORLANDO FVRIOSO DI LVDOVICO ARIOSTO DA
FERRARA ALLO ILLVSTRISSIMO E REVEREN
DISSIMO CARDINALE DONNO HIPPO
IYTO DA ESTE SVO SIGNORE.

CANTO PRIMO.

cerer brings his wits back—in a bottle. He inhales them, regains his sanity, and helps to drive Charlemagne's enemies all the way to Africa.

Tasso's *Gerusalemme liberata* is only slightly less fantastic. Published without his consent in 1581 and spoiled later by the revisions he attempted between attacks of insanity, this epic deals with the First Crusade under Godfrey of Bouillon, a topic it treats as an episodic complex of battles, religious allegories, and love affairs between the knights and pagan heroines, especially Satan's special emissary, the seductively described sorceress Armida.

During this period the once fashionable Portuguese poet Luís vaz de Camões had fallen on evil days, had been arrested for brawling in the street, and had chosen service with the army in India as slightly preferable to jail. During his seventeen unhappy years there Camões wrote *The Lusiads* (1572), a celebration of Portugal's international destiny based on the expedition that Vasco da Gama led to Calicut in 1497–98. In this work the personal heroism of da Gama and his men is expanded to glorify all Portugal, and the expedition's success is made to emblemize the triumph of Christianity and Western culture over paganism—a grand design, with the fashionable romantic addition of a number of passages celebrating women and love.

The epic form is, then, an exaltation of heroic narrative, with the addition of philosophic meanings and moral observations. These elements also exist as forms of their own, of course. The narrative has always been a popular verse form, and Byron's many verse tales, Tennyson's *Idylls of the King*, Pushkin's *Eugene Onegin*, and Hugo's epic-scale *Legend of the Ages* are among the many works that testify to the enduring popularity of such tales throughout the nineteenth century.

The philosophical meditation has had at least as long a career, from the didactic poem *Works and Days*—in which the Greek poet Hesiod, living in the eighth century B.C., takes a lawsuit against his brother as

the occasion for concluding that man must labor all his life, justifying this and other observations by telling us about Prometheus, Pandora, and other myths—through the celebration of Epicurean philosophy by the Roman poet Lucretius in his *On the Nature of Things*, and through Alexander Pope's *Essay on Man*, Tennyson's *In Memoriam*, and T. S. Eliot's *Four Quartets*. With a humorous twist, the moral meditation easily becomes satire, which is equally timeless; and the epic's brief celebrations of beauty, love, and nature—like its laments over old age and death and its longing for better days—have all provided poets with the material for millions of lyric poems.

Material alone, whether for lyric or satire or epic, is not enough, however. Something must be added to turn it into poetry. We are about to follow the course of literary history and see how poet after poet made poetry from these materials, but we cannot put the course before the heart of the matter. We must first ask: What is poetry?

As we have seen, poetry has no necessary connection with specific forms and patterns of verse. In fact it need not be written in verse, and what is written in verse is not therefore poetry. Despite the presence of meter and rhyme, for example, this is not poetry:

COLD BEER

SOLD HERE.

Despite the absence of meter and rhyme, this sentence by Franz Kafka *is* poetry, even in translation: "The hunting dogs are playing in the courtyard, but the hare will not escape them, though even now he is flying through the forest."

Poetry is an honorific term: we use it to praise writing of a certain high intensity. But we also use it to describe the effects of that intensity upon ourselves, and we use it to identify those images and subjects in the outside world that seem to stimulate these effects and this intense writing. One of the best efforts to define this slippery term was made by the English critic William Hazlitt. In part, he said this: "Poetry is the language of the imagination and the passions. It relates to whatever gives immediate pleasure or pain to the human mind. It comes home to the bosoms and businesses of men; for nothing but what so comes home to them in the most general and intelligible shape can be a subject for poetry. Poetry is the universal language which the heart holds with nature and itself. He who has a contempt for poetry cannot have much respect for himself, or for anything else. It is not a mere frivolous accomplishment (as some persons have been led to imagine), the trifling amusement of a few idle readers or leisure hours—it has been the study and delight of mankind in all ages. Many people suppose that poetry is something to be found only in books, contained in lines of ten syllables with like endings: but wherever there is a sense of beauty, or power, or harmony, as in the motion of a wave of the sea, in the growth of a flower that 'spreads its sweet leaves to the air, and dedicates its beauty to the sun,'—*there* is poetry in its birth. If history is a grave study, poetry may be said to be a graver: its materials lie deeper, and are spread wider. History treats, for the most part, of the cumbrous and unwieldy masses of things, the empty cases in which the

Torquato Tasso (above), who like Ariosto enjoyed the patronage of the noble Este family of Ferrara, created his masterpiece, Gerusalemme liberata, *in the luxuriously appointed chamber opposite. In the years that followed, Tasso's physical and mental health deteriorated, and in 1597 the duke of Ferrara felt compelled to commit the poet to an asylum. Released seven years later, Tasso found himself widely acclaimed for his verse.*

affairs of the world are packed, under the heads of intrigue or war, in different states, and from century to century: but there is no thought or feeling that can have entered into the mind of man, which he would be eager to communicate to others, or which they would listen to with delight, that is not a fit subject for poetry. . . . The light of poetry is not only a direct but also a reflected light, that while it shows us the object, throws a sparkling radiance on all around it: the flame of the passions, communicated to the imagination, reveals to us, as with a flash of lightning, the inmost recesses of thought, and penetrates our whole being. Poetry represents forms chiefly as they suggest other forms; feelings, as they suggest forms or other feelings. Poetry puts a spirit of

Roland, the archetype of the steadfast and courageous knight, has been celebrated in French ballads since the ninth century and has been part of that nation's epic literature since the mid-1000s when the Song of Roland *was set down in 4,002 unrhymed lines. A medieval manuscript version of the* Song of Roland *(above) shows the eponymous hero seated among his followers. Opposite, the stalwart paladin and his knights are ambushed in Roncesvalles Pass. Roland's refusal to call for assistance allowed the Saracens to annihilate him and his force.*

life and motion into the universe. . . . It is strictly the language of the imagination; and the imagination is that faculty which represents objects, not as they are in themselves, but as they are moulded by other thoughts and feelings, into an infinite variety of shapes and combinations of power. This language is not the less true to nature, because it is false in point of fact; but so much the more true and natural, if it conveys the impression which the object under the influence of passion makes on the mind. . . ."

Poetry is a troublesome business, however, as well as a satisfying one. The *Song of Roland* tells us that when Charlemagne finds the bodies of Roland and his soldiers on the battlefield, twenty thousand of his barons, overcome with grief, simultaneously swoon. In *The Lusiads* Camões symbolizes Portugal's control of the sea by contriving an Island of Love on which Vasco da Gama's sailors enthusiastically and sensually mate with willing sea nymphs. Vergil introduces us to the hero of his *Aeneid* at an almost comic moment: Aeneas' fleet is being destroyed by a terrible storm, gods are quarreling over him in the heavens, and thunder and lightning have just blasted over the sea. Aeneas is scared stiff:

> At once Aeneas' limbs dissolve with cold;
> He groans, and raises both hands to the sky. . . .

Alexander Pope pretends that the *Essay on Man* is a casual conversation with a nobleman, a chat while strolling around a country estate; and William Wordsworth centers his most ambitious philosophic poem on a traveling peddler.

Poetry has trouble being soberly serious. What began as primitive hooting and childhood play ends up as the most complex, mature, disturbing, and evocative of man's artistic achievements. Yet, at the same time, it is still hooting and play. No wonder it evades our questioning.

2

The Art of Poetry

THE COMPLEX FLOWERING OF WESTERN CULTURE stems from two civilizations; our ancestral tree has two separate roots. We take most of our theology and much of our philosophy from the ancient Hebrew culture, whose primary monument is the Bible; we take much of our philosophy and almost all of our artistic traditions from the varied civilizations that made up the world of ancient Greece. These two sources seem almost unimaginably distant from our mechanized, urbanized, and perplexed society, yet Biblical echoes haunt the writings of T. S. Eliot, the phrases and images of Homer fill Ezra Pound's *Cantos*, and the greatest novel of our century takes its shape and name from the Ithacan king, warrior, and wanderer whom the Romans renamed Ulysses.

Our Hellenic root is itself double, consisting as it does of the Trojan War and Homer's two epics about it, the *Iliad* and the *Odyssey*. Around 1230 B.C., a Greek expeditionary force sacked and burned the semi-Asiatic town of Troy, as other Greeks had done before and as other expeditions would do again. (Modern archaeology suggests that Troy rose and fell a dozen times or so.) This particular attack was probably a major event for the Mycenaean civilization of the Bronze Age, in part because it drew together in an uneasy, temporary alliance so many city-states of the Greek archipelago. But then the years passed; centuries passed; the Iron Age succeeded the Bronze, and Mycenaean civilization went into decline. In the less glorious age that followed, the stories of Mycenae's heyday continued to be told, however, and at some time, perhaps around the end of the eighth century B.C., some bard or bards whom we now call Homer turned to this material, collated it, discarded much of it, and shaped the remainder into two poems that in turn were to shape Western literature.

For Homer to take the Trojan War as his subject was as if a nineteenth-century English poet were to write about King Arthur or Charlemagne (as, in fact, both Milton and Wordsworth did think of doing). Troy was both physically distant—although some scholars think that Homer did visit the site—and historically remote, its heroes and their adventures long ago committed to legend. And it is a measure of the poet's genius that he was able to give them a local habitation and a name, dazzling specificity, and an aura of greatness that in no way obscures their believably human individuality. In addition, he wove these fragmentary stories into two coherent narratives with layers of

31

meaning, complex verbal patterns, and consistent visions of life. Many bards before him had recited stories; Homer raised storytelling to the level of great art.

The *Iliad*, which first was probably called something like *The Wrath of Achilles*, was the earlier poem and for centuries the more popular. Its close focus is remarkable. To take from all the stories of a ten-year siege only those that can be made relevant to Achilles' sulking withdrawal from action during the ninth year and his enraged return after the death of his friend Patroclus; to focus so closely even on this brief time that we see only the highlights against a background of daily warfare; to include the Trojans as equally individual, human, and vivid characters; and—most remarkable of all—to leave untold, though amply prefigured, not only the end of the war but even Achilles' death —all these qualities are evidence of amazing artistic skill, daring, and sophistication on Homer's part, and yet they constitute only a fraction of the success of the poem.

On its surface, the *Iliad* is about war. Much of it deals with battles, and Homer describes the deadly wounds so often, so precisely, and in such detail that long stretches of the poem read like a versified coroner's report after a massacre. Homer's first audiences doubtless listened to the details of fighting and killing with some firsthand knowledge of these necessary arts, and they surely appreciated the expertise displayed. We kill differently now, however, and man-to-man combat seems old-fashioned, tedious, and uneconomically barbaric. As a result we are likely to shy away from the *Iliad* and to condemn Homer unjustly as a warmonger. He was not, however.

Significantly, the horrors of war are deliberately interrupted from time to time by reminders of peaceful struggles, of ordinary men, of natural disasters and minor threats—woodsmen felling trees, herdsmen losing cattle to lions, a world evoked in greater detail by the scenes on Achilles' shield. Such scenes remind us that at heart Homer hates war —its god is "Ares the enemy of humans"—even though most of the *Iliad* demonstrates all too convincingly man's ambivalence toward war, his loathing of it and delight in it, both at once.

At one point in his description of a battle, Homer declares that

Although the Iliad *is, first and foremost, a celebration of the pain and the joy of warfare— its pages filled with vivid descriptions of battle scenes like the one shown in the vase-painting detail above—Homer's narrative is punctuated by many peaceful interludes. During one such pause (right), the warriors Achilles and Ajax seek diversion over a dice table.*

anyone who did not at that moment feel moved by both joy and pain must have been a man of remarkable composure. The pain we understand immediately; the joy of warfare is more difficult, and many people nowadays would rather not believe in it. But Homer knows its power, and that is why the *Iliad* is not basically about war but about glory, the only form of human immortality that really matters, the end-product of the greatest human virtues. The qualities that come near to redeeming war—courage, endurance, piety, honor, pride—are the very qualities that make the poem and the war glorious. For the modern reader those qualities are perhaps best appreciated when he is reminded of what war is like without them, as W.H. Auden has shown in his great poem *The Shield of Achilles*.

Homer knows the joy of battle and of glory. He also knows the pain they cause, and he shows that pain clearly. One of the finest qualities of the *Iliad* is that everyone is given his due, from the grim heroes pitilessly hacking their way to fame, through the victimized wives and children, down to the pitiable slave women who weep over the body of Patroclus but who actually bewail their own destinies and not his death. Perhaps only Nestor, the hero of earlier battles who has outlived his fate and his glory and who now babbles on in wise senility—only Nestor, the antithesis of the doomed Achilles, fails to be redeemed by Homer's clear-eyed understanding.

The *Iliad's* narrative tone has been described as "inhuman calm." This calm persists even while Homer describes the grimmest battlefield deaths, and it stoops to commentary only in such practical matters as genealogy and the assertion that mules are better for plowing than oxen are. Showing both the joy and the pain of life, Homer does not break up his lines to weep, making the *Iliad* perhaps the most tough-minded work of literature in the world. The *Odyssey* is its complement. In the *Iliad* Homer celebrated the glory of glory by ratifying Achilles' choice of a brief and famous life rather than a long and obscure one. But in the *Odyssey*, Achilles has found a new wisdom akin to the bleak wisdom of Ecclesiastes' "a living dog is better than a dead lion." When Odysseus meets the spirit of Achilles in Hades he exclaims:

> "No man in the past or hereafter is more blessed than you.
> When you were alive before, the Argives honored you
> Equal to the gods. Now you greatly rule over the dead,
> Being here as you are. So do not grieve now you are dead,
>   Achilles."
> Thus I spoke, and he at once addressed me in answer:
> "Noble Odysseus, do not commend death to me.
> I would rather serve on the land of another man
> Who had no portion and not a great livelihood
> Than to rule over all the shades of those who are dead."

The change is almost total. Homer now chooses for his hero not another doomed and single-minded killer but rather a sly trickster, a clever man who uses his wits to stay alive. The *Odyssey* constitutes quite a promotion for Odysseus, whose rank among the warriors in the *Iliad* is suggested by his small army: Agamemnon's fleet consisted of

one hundred and sixty ships; Achilles', fifty; Odysseus', only twelve.
Only two of the twenty-one armies were smaller than his, but what he
lacked in rank and steadfast heroism he more than compensated for by
his many other qualities, qualities that once led James Joyce to describe
him as the only "complete all-round character presented by any
writer." "Ulysses is son to Laertes," Joyce said, "but he is father to
Telemachus, husband to Penelope, lover of Calypso, companion in arms
of the Greek warriors around Troy, and King of Ithaca. He was sub-
jected to many trials, but with wisdom and courage came through them
all. Don't forget that he was a war dodger who tried to evade military
service by simulating madness. He might never have taken up arms and
gone to Troy, but the Greek recruiting sergeant was too clever for
him, and while he was ploughing the sands, placed young Telemachus
in front of his plough. But . . . when the others wanted to abandon the
siege he insisted on staying till Troy should fall."

This completeness of character is revealed to us by the many adventures summed up in the opening lines of the poem:

> Tell me, Muse, about the man of many turns, who many
> Ways wandered when he had sacked Troy's holy citadel;
> He saw the cities of many men, and he knew their thought;
> On the ocean he suffered many pains within his heart,
> Striving for his life and his companions' return.

But the many cities and seas where Odysseus finds suffering and adventure are not simply the scenes of unrelated episodic events, as in a pica-
resque novel. Each is a test of character and a source of knowledge; all
serve Odysseus as definers of his name and fame. And name and fame
are what the *Odyssey* is all about.

In the adventure with the one-eyed giant Polyphemos, Odysseus
puns on his name and calls himself Outis, "nobody." But when he has

blinded the ogre and he and his crew are making their escape, he risks death in order to let the world know who he is:

> Cyclops, if someone among mortal men should inquire
> Of you about the unseemly blindness in your eye,
> Say that Odysseus, sacker of cities, blinded it,
> The son of Laertes, whose home is in Ithaca.

The episode is characteristic. Here, as with each danger, Odysseus risks his fame, risks becoming a nobody. He must repeatedly avoid oblivion by making a name for himself. The opium temptations of Lotus-land, the idle and sophisticated superficiality of the Phaeacians, the sensual animality of Circe's sty, and the romantic dalliance with Calypso all pose the same threat, a threat implicit in Calypso's name and echoed verbally throughout the poem. Calypso comes from *kalypsein*, meaning to cover over, to smother, to swallow up. The cave of Polyphemos, the embraces of Calypso and Circe, the dark shadows of Hades, and the vast ocean itself all threaten to cover Odysseus with oblivion—not merely death, of which he has little fear, but namelessness. Not to be a nobody, but to be alive and a hero: that is his consuming ambition.

For English-speaking readers the heroism of the *Oydssey* has often

For centuries after their composition the Iliad *and the* Odyssey *remained the chief source of inspiration for Greek artisans of every variety. The face that launched a thousand ships graces the krater fragment seen below, and Odysseus' temptation by the Sirens is imaginatively depicted in the fifth-century* B.C. *vase painting at left. A potter from Rhodes, mining the same thematic lode a century earlier, transformed the utilitarian amphora (right) into the bust of a helmeted warrior.*

been so watered down by conventional translators that it seems to consist simply of piety and endurance; in fact it is a fierce and frightening matter. In Greek the name Odysseus means, roughly, trouble, suffering, and hostility—and has a double reference. Odysseus is certainly a victim of suffering, as the poem's opening makes clear, but he is also a continuous causer of pain. His first act after leaving Troy is to sack the city of Ismaros, loot the town, kill its men, and enslave its women. He saddens Calypso and Nausicaa by leaving them behind; his visit ruins life for the Phaeacians; he blinds Polyphemos; and, upon his return to Ithaca, he puts to death more than a hundred suitors and a dozen slave women. Pain is a condition of life for Odysseus, and the cost of being somebody instead of nobody is perpetual risk, suffering, and conquest.

What makes him an epic hero and not merely another piratical destroyer of life and property is that his trouble, both inflicted and suffered, brings with it wisdom. The Phaeacians, distant from pain, possess a worldly sophistication that allows them to laugh at the gods, especially at the minstrel Demodocus' tale of Hephaestos catching his wife Aphrodite with her lover Ares. Menelaus and Helen also live elegant lives, and their memories of the Trojan War cheapen it to subtle games and odd experiences on the way home. Nestor is a wise man, but in his

extreme old age his wisdom is like that of Polonius, fixed and aphoristic. It is useful for boys like Telemachos but is inadequate for the fullest life. Odysseus takes us beyond these shallow and incomplete forms of knowledge and experience, takes us from encounters with gods to explorations of Hades. And if the poem concludes in no explicitly stated wisdom, that is because we have learned that wisdom cannot be caught and frozen in words but must be acted out, in the midst of suffering, so long as we live.

The Greeks taught morality and ethical behavior by example: in the *Iliad* Achilles is warned against stubbornness by the story of Meleager, and in the *Odyssey* Telemachos is repeatedly urged to act against the suitors by being reminded of Orestes' recent vengeance, a case that even Zeus found instructive. The Homeric epics contain a wealth of these good and bad examples, so clearly imagined and vividly expressed that both works remained at the center of Greek education for a thousand years. But they are works of art, not mere manuals of instruction, and art is always troublesome.

Homer's ideals are aristocratic: his heroes are skilled in hand-to-hand combat, eloquence, athletic skills, and courtesy. They are brave, blond, and handsome, and they descend from historically important families and from the gods themselves. But in the developing democratic city-states of Greece, especially in Sparta and Athens, such haughty and individualistic values were as irrelevant as knights at a town meeting. What was now needed was a coherent, disciplined, self-sacrificing citizenry, loyal to the state above themselves and seeking not personal glory but communal well-being. Citizenship and civic

Homer's chronological successor was the lyric poet and satirist Archilochus, a mercenary soldier turned versifier who had experienced firsthand the sort of combat depicted on the kylix at lower left. Homer had glorified the warrior, and other Greek artists—the creator of the bronze helmet fitting at right, above, among them— had followed suit. War-weary Archilochus could not, and his verses are filled with bitterly antiheroic sentiment. The poet Pindar (right, below) often composed odes in praise of victorious athletes.

approval, both available to the common man, now became the esteemed virtues. The conservative Athenian poet Pindar (c. 518–438) might still write complex odes in which winners of the Olympic games were praised as if they ranked with Achilles and Odysseus, but the Spartan military poet Tyrtaeus, in his much-quoted and imitated poems about discipline, collective bravery, and patriotic efforts, spoke for one form of the democratic future. Another form, in which the individual reacts against his public role and insists on his private self, produced the sentimental lyrics of Sappho and the skeptical antiheroism of Archilochus. The latter, a mercenary soldier, knew all the heroic talk about returning from battle with one's shield or on it, but he reacted much like the cynical Thersites of Homer's *Iliad*:

> Well, what if some barbaric Thracian glories
> in the perfect shield I left under a bush?
> I was sorry to leave it—but I saved my skin.
> Does it matter? O hell, I'll get a better one.

The abrupt skepticism, faultfinding, and insistence on moderation in Archilochus' poems have little power to stir us now, yet the Greeks ranked him with Homer as a source of public instruction. Meanwhile, Achilles and Odysseus were fitting awkwardly into the curriculum—Achilles, who refused to fight for the united Greek cause out of rage at the loss of his personal glory; and Odysseus, who survived by trickery and guile, even at the expense of his crew. The *Odyssey* itself came to be treated as a novel, not as a truthful epic, and one learned from selected passages in it rather than from the work as a whole. As for Achilles, he remained a significant example, but a negative one: his fate teaches us not to disobey our country, not to put our private self ahead of our role as citizen.

Through all this the epic remained the best and most memorable form in which to express the examples and events on which so much ethical teaching depended. Even the decay of Greek power and the westward movement of civilization did not weaken its influence, which survived unabated when the city-states of Greece collapsed and the semibarbarous state of Rome assumed control of the Mediterranean world. As Rome took its empire from the Greeks, so it took its culture; writers, dramatists, historians, musicians, painters, sculptors, architects—all stole extensively from their Greek predecessors.

Julius Caesar changed Rome from a fierce and strife-ridden republic into an expanding, cosmopolitan empire-machine. His assassination in 44 B.C. plunged that empire into chaos and civil war, as Shakespeare shows so vividly in *Julius Caesar* and *Antony and Cleopatra*. Mark Antony's subsequent defeat at Actium in 31 B.C. left the empire in the hands of Octavian, Caesar's nephew and ward, who took on the politically numinous name of Augustus Caesar and consolidated Rome's political and military power. Until his death in A.D. 14 Augustus was to preside over the most polished and prolific era in the history of Latin poetry. There had been great Roman poets before his time—notably Catullus and Lucretius—and some of the sharpest satirists, men such as Martial, Juvenal, and Petronius, were yet to come. Indeed, Catullus was the

Under the aegis of Augustus Caesar, whose imperial profile adorns the sardonyx cameo at left, Latin poetry was to reach its greatest heights. The outstanding didactic poem of the period was Vergil's Georgics, *a paean to rural life. Seven years in the writing, this poetic response to Lucretius'* On the Nature of Things *was very loosely based upon an earlier Greek classic, Hesiod's* Works and Days. *An illuminated page from a sixth-century A.D. manuscript version of the* Georgics *is reproduced at right.*

greatest lyric poet in the language, and his poems, like those of the satirists, have been imitated and pillaged down through the ages. But when we think of Roman literature it is of Augustan Rome that we think, of Vergil and Horace, of Propertius and Ovid.

Augustus liked to boast that he found Rome brick and left it marble. He was right, at least about his effect on poetry. Lucretius' *On the Nature of Things* is moderate and dignified in tone, although it sinks occasionally to satire and rises often to considerable eloquence; and Catullus writes a lively personal style that persistently defies translation. But neither poet is elegant, refined, perfect. It was Augustus' desire to outdo the Greeks—and his notion that the way to do this was to be finer—that led Roman poetry to develop its marmoreal splendors. Poetry also devoted itself to civic service with a patriotic fervor it would not display again until the rise of the Soviet Union.

The end of the civil war left Rome militarily strong but sadly in need of morale boosting and moral improvement. What is more, Augustus needed propaganda that would advertise the strength and validity of his rule and celebrate the significance and legitimacy of Rome in the Mediterranean world, changing the city's image from that of an upstart barbarian encampment to that of a destined heir of culture, the favored city of the gods. Given the importance of poetry, it was almost a foregone conclusion that he would turn to his old acquaintance and favorite court poet, Publius Vergilius Maro (70–19 B.C.), and commission him to write an epic. It was equally predictable that Vergil would turn immediately to Homer and that he would display true Roman ambition by modeling his *Aeneid* on the *Odyssey* and the *Iliad* both. (Even Propertius briefly felt a patriotic glow: "Give up, you Roman writers! Quit, you Greeks!" he wrote; "something greater than the *Iliad* is being born!")

Vergil was a mild and unmilitary man, a central figure in the fashionable literary circles of Rome but inclined to prefer the country, about which he had written his bucolic *Eclogues* and *Georgics*. (The first of these was a collection of polished tales of equally polished pastoral life, imitating the Sicilian Greek pastoral poets Theocritus and Bion; the second, a collection of pseudodidactic poems on farming,

these also elegant and artificial.) He was therefore by no means an obvious choice to produce Augustus' epic, except in his degree of poetic skill, and not surprisingly his *Aeneid* is the most refined and most emotional of epics. It also undercuts almost all of the traditional epic virtues. The second half, which no one much likes, is modeled on the *Iliad* and recounts Aeneas' campaign to take over Italy and plant his colony of Trojans there. The topic is uncongenial to Vergil's peaceful muse, and she displays her pacifism by making Aeneas an unattractive bully and Turnus, his doomed opponent, romantically interesting.

In the much better first half, readers are struck especially by such unepical scenes as Aeneas' display of fear in the midst of a storm at sea, his passionate night in the cave with Dido, her wild lament at his desertion, and her stony silence when they meet again in Hades. The brief passages that have been quoted down through the centuries are equally unheroic: they include Dido's "not ignorant of grief, I know how to aid the afflicted"; Laocoön's "I fear the Greeks, even when bearing gifts"; Aeneas' "there are tears even in things, and mortal matters touch the mind"; and many more, culminating in the lament on the death of

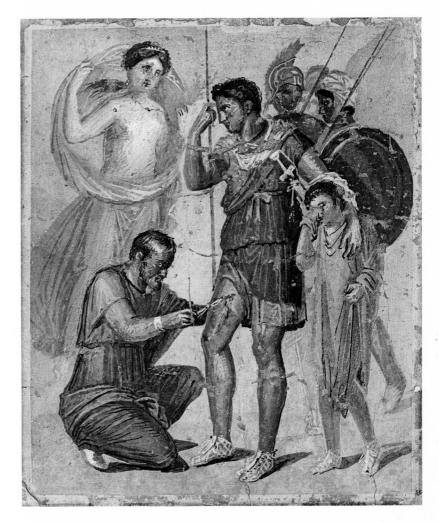

Marcellus, which Vergil himself recited to the boy's mother and her brother Augustus. Tradition has it that she swooned away, and that later she presented the poet with ten thousand sesterces for each of the affecting lines.

Aeneas is no Greek hero, ambitious of glory. His repeated epithet is "pious," and he is. He is a good father and a good son, reluctant to fight, dutiful, prudent, and in all ways a model of Augustus' favorite moral cliché, the golden mean. For that reason the proud rhetorical passage in which Anchises predicts the coming glories of Augustan Rome closes somberly. The triumphs of art are mentioned only to be relegated to more fortunate civilizations, and Rome's political glory is hedged about with prudence, moderation, and justice:

> Others will forge more gracefully breathing bronzes
> and draw from the marble living visages:
> plead causes better at court, and point out wisely
> the heavenly motions and the surging stars:
> yours to rule the nations, Rome, with empire:
> these are your arts: to set the terms of peace,
> to spare the conquered and beat down the proud.

The *Aeneid* was famous even before it was written, and although it

is said that the dying Vergil asked that it be burned as incomplete, there was no chance that Augustus would relinquish a work at once so grand and so useful. It took a central place in the Roman educational system, and hundreds of years later it was still studied for its information on Roman and Mediterranean history. The readers of the Middle Ages were fond of finding allegories everywhere, and the *Aeneid* became a favorite source: Vergil was taken to be a holy magician, Aeneas' adventures were allegorized as the soul's troubles, and people seeking advice used the *Aeneid* as they do the *I-Ching*, opening the

The Aeneid was indisputably epic in form, but its protagonist was anything but epic in demeanor. More human than godlike, more prudent than ambitious, Aeneas was to reveal altogether understandable terror during a storm at sea (above) and too-human frailty during his encounter with the seductive Carthaginian queen Dido (right).

44

volume at random and sticking a pin randomly into a line of verse. It was as poet, philosopher, and prophet that Dante Alighieri read him and chose him as guide through Hell. The magic later wore off, but by the sixteenth century Vergil had become the greatest figure in classical literature, and when European civilization strove to re-create Augustan values they turned especially to Vergil as a model.

They also turned to Horace (65–8 B.C.), Vergil's contemporary and his equivalent in smaller verse forms. Horace had backed the wrong side in the civil war, as many writers had, but he was a practical man, and broke, and therefore willing to write in the Augustan mode. Under the liberal patronage of Maecenas, who also subsidized Vergil, Propertius, and several other poets, he became a major spokesman for gentlemanliness, the golden mean, and poetic law and order. Toward the end of his life Horace versified most of his central literary precepts in a casual poem for some acquaintances, a poem taken as law by later ages, retitled *The Art of Poetry*, and imitated exhaustively, especially by the French poet Nicolas Boileau and by Alexander Pope, whose *Essay on Criticism* reads like a translation of Horace—and often is.

Another contemporary of Horace and Vergil is more to our contemporary taste. Sextus Propertius (49–15 B.C.), born in Verona but later joining a sophisticated Roman literary group, followed the Greek lyricist Callimachus in his use of complex prosodic forms and imitated his great predecessor Catullus in writing repeatedly about his head-over-heels involvement with an unmanageable woman. Most of the verse that Propertius poured out in his short life deals with his varied and harried wooing of Cynthia, a counterpart of Catullus' Lesbia. Catullus had summed up his exasperated relationship with Lesbia in the epigram

> I hate and I love: you ask why the hell I do it?
> Damned if I know; I'm in hell, I'm driven to it.

Propertius' poems never reach Catullus' extremes of ecstasy and vulgarity, but Ezra Pound's modern imitations of him show that he was far from being dully moderate:

> Yet you ask on what account I write so many love-lyrics
> And whence this soft book comes into my mouth.
> Neither Calliope nor Apollo sung these things into my ear,
>   My genius is no more than a girl.
>
> If she with ivory fingers drive a tune through the lyre,
>   We look at the process.
> How easy the moving fingers; if hair is mussed on her forehead,
> If she goes in a gleam of Cos, in a slither of dyed stuff,
> There is a volume in the matter; if her eyelids sink into sleep,
> There are new jobs for the author;
> And if she plays with me with her shirt off,
>   We shall construct many Iliads.
> And whatever she does or says
>   We shall spin long yarns out of nothing. . . .

Another Augustan poet combined the lyric gifts of Propertius with a far wider scope and an enormous output. For hundreds of years he displaced or rivaled Vergil as the greatest of Roman poets, and since Latin has always been more widely known than Greek—even after its disappearance as a spoken language—he ranked for a time as the second-best poet of the Western world. Few now read Publius Ovidius Naso (43 B.C.–c. A.D. 17), yet this fellow poet to Vergil, Horace, Tibullus, and Propertius remains as charming, polished, interesting, and wittily erotic as ever. Petrarch and Boccaccio in Italy; Goethe in Germany;

If Vergil was primus inter pares *in Augustan literary circles, it was only because his vision encompassed all of Roman history. Horace, whose scope was more restricted, was recognized as the master of the ode, as* The Carmina *(above), a collection published in 23* B.C., *attests.*

Ronsard, Montaigne, Molière, and Racine in France; and Chaucer, Shakespeare, Milton, Dryden, Wordsworth, Landor, and Swinburne in England all read him with profit and delight, and a passage from his *Metamorphoses* stands as epigraph to Joyce's *Portrait of the Artist as a Young Man*. Readers through the ages have been delighted with the flood of elegantly retold myths that make up the *Metamorphoses*; and most of them have found equal if less readily admitted amusement in the *Loves* and the *Art of Love*.

In the *Loves* the young Ovid pretends to give his erotic autobiography, which serves as an excuse for stringing together practically every kind of amorous relationship and feeling: passion, jealousy, lust, impotence, success, failure, anger, despair, hope, and wit. But here as elsewhere, even in the *Art of Love*, Ovid displays a characteristic rarely found in "libertine" men: he understands women, he sympathizes with them, and he shows them realistically, clearly, and unromantically. This alone is enough to recommend him to us, and his witty practicality about sex and love—neither swooning nor leering—completes his relevance. His *Art of Love* is neither didactic nor pornographic. It pretends to be a versified treatise such as were often written on the most unpromising of subjects, but it is actually an amusing compendium of observations on flirting, chasing, and captivating, written for an audience as sophisticated, self-indulgent, and clever as that of Restoration London. The first book tells how to find and catch a mistress; the second tells how to keep her; the third—characteristically—is addressed to women and gives them advice on the same subjects.

The more respectable great work of his maturity, the *Metamorphoses*, is longer than the *Aeneid* and contains over fifty extended stories as well as hundreds of brief ones. Not all deal with actual metamorphosis, although all put together may be thought of as tracing the world's evolution from its creation through the founding of Rome and that city's metamorphosis under Augustus from a city of bricks to one of marble. The stories are written in a style of high-class amusement and gilded with witty observations from which the gods suffer no less than men. Whether funny or pathetic the stories are swiftly and vividly told, and for centuries they have been stolen or imitated by poets and painters alike.

Old or young, in favor or exile, in major or minor works, Ovid is the liveliest, wittiest, and most inventive of poets. The priggish Augustus had him banished from Rome and his books removed from the public libraries, perhaps because he wished to blame the *Art of Love* for having provoked the repeated adulteries of his daughter and her daughter. But other copies remained and other generations remained to read and praise them. For eleven centuries Ovid's exile continued—the Catholic Church thought of him much as Augustus had—and then, finally, he returned to delight generations of readers who could cherish this world as well as the world to come. These readers popularized him on occasion even with the Establishment, so that once King James I of Aragon began a speech to a group of barons and bishops with a quotation that he thought was from the Bible, but that actually was from the *Art of Love*.

3

New Poets, New Tongues

SURROUNDED BY OUR SOLID MACHINES and our metal cities we easily disbelieve that civilization can ever end. Yet when marble Rome collapsed as the monumental Greek world had previously done, Western civilization very nearly collapsed with it. Rome's ruins remained, of course, like those of Egypt, Athens, Alexandria, Stonehenge, and Knocknarea—and shepherds watching their flocks nearby invented stories of giants and gods to explain those shattered buildings, so plainly beyond the power of living men to construct. Christianity remained too, and the clergy used those ruins as evidence that the material world was soon to end, that life was ephemeral and eternity at hand, and that sensible people should keep foremost in mind the Four Last Things: death, judgment, heaven, and hell.

Life went on. The sun shone and rain fell. People were born, loved, failed or prospered, aged, sickened, and died. And, as always, these events were celebrated or lamented in verse, some of it still readable and affecting today. But the language itself was dying; the great unified empire of the Latin language was collapsing into the Tower-of-Babel diversity from which we still suffer. When poetry rose again, one of its chief monuments was written in Italian, not Latin, and concerned itself not with this passing world but with the Four Last Things and the eternity to come.

Dante Alighieri (1265–1321) honored Homer, Horace, and Ovid by placing them among the great pagan dead in Limbo, and he made Vergil his guide through Hell and Purgatory; but the *Commedia, The Divine Comedy,* is essentially different from their poetry and from any we have seen so far. In the *Iliad* and the *Odyssey* the gods are important, certainly, but Achilles and Hector preoccupy us with their fated varieties of glory, and Odysseus is unquestionably worth the attention of the gods. The *Aeneid* is different, and it points the way toward its Italian successor: pious Aeneas is less skillful and glorious than his Greek models; he is merely a forceful administrator, a responsible executive burdened by his destiny. It is what he represents that ennobles him; he embodies the entire Roman Empire. Then that empire fell, and the advent of Christianity hastened what democratic ideas and large cities had begun—a diminution of the importance of human individuality. People learned to think primarily of types and groups: pagans and Christians, the damned and the saved.

At this point the meaning of life also changes. In the Greek epics, it inheres in the individual heroes and their actions. In the *Aeneid*, all the suffering, voyaging, and fighting are justified by something that does not even appear directly in the poem, something that would not result from these actions for hundreds of years—the empire. In Dante's *Commedia*, significance has become still more detached from the poem's action; it is the shape God has given to the whole of existence. The characters and events of the poem cause nothing, create nothing; they only reveal or have revealed to them this God-given meaning.

By Dante's time Catholicism had accepted the idea that God had written two books, the Bible and the world. Both contained His thought and His truths, although the fall of Adam and Eve had marred the physical world and had blurred its reflection of heavenly thought. Since the artist imitates God the creator, a proper work of art ought to reflect unblurred the structure of the world; its form should teach just as its content does. For Dante a central truth of Catholicism was the doctrine that God is one being in three persons: the Father, the Son, and the Holy Ghost—power, wisdom, and love. This doctrine contains many implications, and for the medieval churchmen whom Dante studied, a number of these implications were mathematical.

When he had almost finished the *Commedia* Dante wrote a long letter to his patron Can Grande della Scala in which he explained some of the sense and structure of his poem. One of his first points was that the poem has many meanings: it has a literal meaning, and it also has meanings that he classified as allegoric, moral, and mystical—that is, three meanings contained within one. The *Commedia* also has three parts—the *Inferno*, the *Purgatorio*, and the *Paradiso*—forming one whole. Each part contains thirty-three cantos (three times eleven), with an introductory canto bringing the total to the perfect number 100. The cantos are written in three-line stanzas, and each canto ends with a single line. The rhyme form, which Dante devised, employs sequences of three rhymes, each of which appears three times. Beyond this, the Inferno itself is composed of a vestibule plus the nine circles of Hell; the climb to the top of the Mount of Purgatory takes three days and nights and ends with one morning in the Earthly Paradise; and the nine heavens of Paradise lead us to the one all-controlling Empyrean. Dante even carries this one-and-three scheme to the length of setting the poem's events in the year 1300.

This mathematical construction—of which we have barely scratched the surface—supports a landscape that Dante has imagined with unsurpassed vividness and detail, and the landscape itself is consistently meaningful. The funnel-shaped hole of Hell is the horrific reverse image of the conical Mount of Purgatory; the dangerous and difficult climb down through Hell is set against the exuberant flight from sphere to sphere in Paradise. As Dante informed Can Grande, "Everything that moves has some defect, and does not grasp its whole being at once." Correspondingly, Hell and Paradise are timeless, because their inhabitants are damnably or blessedly perfect; Purgatory exists in time, as the sinners expiate their faults from year to year and level to level.

So thoroughly does Dante know and believe in this landscape that it

52

In his autobiographical poem, La Vita Nuova, Dante examined his deep and unrequited love for Beatrice Portinari. Upon completing that work, Dante vowed to write no more about her until he could say "what hath not before been written of any woman." He magnificently fulfilled this vow in The Divine Comedy, in which Beatrice is his guide through Purgatory and into Paradise. The details at left, illustrations from a rare edition of the poem, show the last place of exile for Dante and Beatrice before they enter Paradise (below) and a portrait of Beatrice (above). At right, Dante and Vergil observe a storm cloud sweeping away the misers.

controls even his metaphors. In the *Purgatorio*, for instance, he is repeatedly told not to expect complete understanding, because the deepest knowledge is too far beneath the ocean for man to perceive it. Then, when he arrives in Paradise and looks fixedly at his blessed guide Beatrice, he tells us that he feels like the simple fisherman Glaucus when he tasted the divine food "which made him able to consort with the other Gods under the ocean." And, sure enough, Dante is suddenly able to dive down to those deepest truths in Paradise.

Again in the *Purgatorio*, Dante's first meeting with Beatrice proves to be no sentimental reunion: she is furious with him for having forgotten her and having turned to other wisdom and other women after her death. The poet's reaction to her scolding is a horrible coldness in his heart. The reaction seems only natural, but the reader remembers the sinners at the very bottom of the Inferno: they too were faithless, and they too are frozen to the heart. Such coherence and consistency of detail have an amazing power over the reader. He is in a world totally separate from his ordinary experience, and yet Dante's testimony is so vivid and unified that even the non-Italian, non-Christian reader finds the journey though the *Commedia* hauntingly persuasive.

At the same time it must be admitted that comparatively few readers make the whole trip. T. S. Eliot offers one ironic reason: "It is apparently easier to accept damnation as poetic material than purgation or beatitude; less is involved that is strange to the modern mind." Dante himself offers another reason. Just arrived in Paradise and looking forward to the difficult truths he must express, he addresses his readers as ironically as Eliot:

> O you there in your tiny boats,
> > wanting to listen, who have followed
> > behind my ship as it has sailed and sung,
> Turn back to your own shores;

don't set out on that sea where, perhaps,
losing track of me, you might be lost.

The *Commedia* rises not only from Hell to Paradise but from men to man and then to spirit. In addition, it rises from doubts and questions to answers and perfect faith. The answers are difficult, but doubt is easy—and perfection, even in the *Commedia*, cannot hold our attention like the intensely imperfect individuals of Hell and the early stages of Purgatory. Yet we owe it to Dante and ourselves, even if we read only the *Inferno*, to see it as part of a grand whole. Take, for instance, our arrival in Hell, and the Hell-gate inscription that no humane person can read undismayed:

Through me one goes into the grieving city,
   through me one goes into eternal grief,
      through me one goes among the damned people.
Justice moved my high maker;
   I was created by divine power,
      the highest wisdom and the primal love.
Before me no created things existed
   but those eternal, and I exist eternally.
      Abandon every hope, you who enter.

Eternal damnation in itself is difficult to accept, and the notion that Hell was built by love seems a gratuitous insult to God. Dante makes our acceptance more difficult: although Homer is celebrated among the pagan poets in Limbo, Homer's heroes are damned: Achilles, for love of Patroclus, now whirls endlessly in the wind; and Odysseus, despite the heroic love of knowledge Dante gives him, burns as a tongue of flame for his lying tongue. God's justice is not sugarcoated for us; on the contrary, we must struggle to understand it.

The Dante who leads us through the Inferno understands all this no better than we do, and his limitations cause him to succumb repeatedly to the sins he encounters. Leaving the damned whose sin is anger, Dante is angry; leaving the hypocrites, he pretends to be stronger than he feels; among the faithless, he makes a bargain with a sinner and then betrays him. But the wiser Dante who wrote the *Commedia* is not susceptible; he understands all this, and so he can show us that the damned are self-condemned. They love their sin; even in Hell they will not give it up. The deceitful, the angry, the sullen are still so now, despite their self-inflicted pain; and if we sympathize, we risk the same fate.

According to Dante's understanding of psychology, every human must love. What we love determines what we are. It shapes our psyche, and we may become godlike by loving God as we should, or horribly perverse, misshapen, and self-torturing, like the souls in Hell, if we love what corrupts us. It is especially in this sense that love has built the Inferno, and it built Purgatory and Paradise as well—although the closer we come to God the more completely our desire matches His, so that the individual and willful sufferings of Hell are replaced by the general beatitude in which all the souls of Paradise unite in self-abnegation: "In His will is our peace."

An imperious, hawk-nosed Dante dominates the elaborate title page (above) of an edition of his collected works published in Venice in 1578. The illustration of Hell at left appeared as the frontispiece of an early edition of The Divine Comedy. *From several points in the picture Dante, dressed in a red robe, and his guide Vergil, in blue, survey the tormented souls. At bottom, the three-headed figure of Satan consumes the souls of the traitors Judas, Brutus, and Cassius.*

It is a long journey from the dark wood of human error to that final knowledge of "the love that moves the Sun and the other stars." Thanks to the *Commedia*, it may be taken allegorically by every man, every soul, every lover seeking a proper object of desire; but it was first taken by Dante, who began life as an aspiring poet and politician amid the political and religious strife of the brawling thirteenth-century city-state of Florence, serving his city as soldier and governor and serving his chosen muse, Beatrice Portinari, as poet and platonic lover. Latin was still the proper language of literature then, but under Beatrice's influence, or so Dante says, he joined with other young poets in devising a "sweet new style" of verse in Italian, modeled on that of the Provençal troubadours and elaborately formalized and intellectualized. Even in translation the beauty of the Italian *canzoni* he wrote can be sensed, as in this opening stanza of a sestina:

> To brief day and the great circle of shade
> I have come, alas! and the hills' whitening,
> when all the color in the grass is lost.
> Yet my desire does not change its green,
> so rooted is it in the solid stone
> that speaks and hears as if it were a woman.

But meanwhile the saving tragedy of Dante's life had occurred. Tangled in increasingly bitter political feuds, he represented Florence in an embassy sent to Pope Boniface VIII in 1302. He was returning from this journey when, in Siena, he heard that he had been banished from Florence. He never saw his beloved city again.

Exile was misery for Dante—a misery that the *Commedia* often echoes—but it was while wandering from city to city and patron to patron that he set himself the incredible task of rising up from his own concerns and his shattered life to a point from which he could see everything, understand it, and, by accepting it, transform it from misery to comedy. That he was able to achieve this outlook is perhaps even more impressive than the poem he made of the achievement. Homer had sung of individual heroes; Vergil had celebrated the establishment of the Roman Empire; but Dante, as he told Can Grande, took as his subject "the condition of souls after death" literally, and allegorically "man, as by his good or bad deserving, from his own freedom of choice, he has earned reward or punishment from justice." Not Achilles, not the Romans, but *man*: few poets have aspired so high.

It is love that makes the world go round. Dante made that clear—as both Lucretius and Ovid had done many centuries before him. But in the Middle Ages love began to rival war and heroism as a major topic of poetry. Verse narratives abounded, from the *Romance of the Rose* through hundreds of lays, tales, allegories, dream visions, and romantic idylls, and most of them touched on love or dwelt on it. *Aucassin and Nicolette*—part prose and part verse—told a charmingly false-naïve French story of successful love; the stories of Tristan and Isolde turned the theme to tragedy; and all the variations in between were developed in song and story. Perhaps never before or since were women so important in poetry, whether as realistic, witty, and thoroughly practical

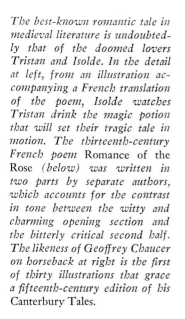

The best-known romantic tale in medieval literature is undoubtedly that of the doomed lovers Tristan and Isolde. In the detail at left, from an illustration accompanying a French translation of the poem, Isolde watches Tristan drink the magic potion that will set their tragic tale in motion. The thirteenth-century French poem Romance of the Rose *(below) was written in two parts by separate authors, which accounts for the contrast in tone between the witty and charming opening section and the bitterly critical second half. The likeness of Geoffrey Chaucer on horseback at right is the first of thirty illustrations that grace a fifteenth-century edition of his* Canterbury Tales.

pleasure-seekers or as idealized, exalted, and allegorized mistress-muses such as Dante's Beatrice and Petrarch's Laura. And no one since Ovid has played more and better variations on this great theme than that frenchified English diplomat, scholar, and man of the world Geoffrey Chaucer (c. 1340–1400).

Dante's *Commedia*, like some of the great Buddhist shrines, begins with vivid images of sensual existence and then rises upward to the imageless purity of clear light. Chaucer's comedies keep their feet planted firmly on the ground. And what a lively and crowded ground it is! In *The Canterbury Tales* Chaucer moves among more than two dozen tale-telling pilgrims as Dante moved among the intense Italians of the *Commedia*, listening, commenting, portraying himself in a mildly comic fashion, and even taking part in the action. Yet the effect could hardly be more different. There is no form to the *Tales* except that given by the pilgrims' agreement to tell stories on the way to the shrine of St. Thomas à Becket and back to London. Indeed, the *Tales* were never completed—that would have required over a hundred stories— and they do not rise toward the heavens. It is true that heavenly love is evoked early in them: in the *Prologue* we are told that the Prioress wears a brooch inscribed "Love conquers all." She is a very worldly, vain, and dressy young prioress, however, and we have our doubts about that brooch. Our doubts—and Chaucer's—extend to most of the Church's representatives and their loves: the Monk loves hunting, the Friar loves dalliance, the Summoner loves drink and lechery, and the strange Pardoner is apparently in love with evil itself. Only the simple Priest is wholeheartedly praised. "He was a shepherd and not a mercenary," Chaucer says:

> The lore of Christ and his Apostles twelve
> He taught, but first he followed it himself.

Whan þat Aprill wyth his schoures soote
Ye droughte of March haþ perced to þe roote
And baþid euery veyne in suche lycoure
Of whiche vertue engendred is þe floure
Whan zephirus eke wyth his swete breþe
Inspired haþ in euery holte & heþe
The tendre croppes & þe yonge sonne
Haþe in þe ram his half cours ronne
And smal foules maken melodye
þat slepen alle nyght wyþ open yhe
So prikleþ hem nature in þer corages
Than longen folke to gone one pilgrimages
And palmeres for to seeke straungeir stroudes
To ferne halowes cowþe in sundre londes
And specially from euery schyres ende
Of Ingelonde to Canterburi þei wende
The holy blisful martyr for to seke
Þat hem haþ holpen whan þei were seke
It befil þan in þat seson vpon a daie
In Suthewerke att ye tabard as I laie
Redi to wende on my pilgremage
To canterburie wyþ ful devoute corage
Att nyghte was come in to þat hostellerie
Wel nyne and twente in a companye
Of sondre folke be aventure yfalle
In felauschipe & Pilgrimes were þei alle
To warde canterburi þat wolde ride
The chambres & stables weren wyde
And wele weren esede att þe beste
An schortly whan þe son was to reste
So had I spoken wyþ hem euerichone
þat I was of her felawschipe anone
And made forward erly for to rise
To take owre waie þer as I yowe devise
But napeles while I haue tyme & space
Er þat I ferþer in þis tale pace
Me þenkeþ it accordant to resone
To tell yowe all þe condicione
Of iche of hem so as it semed me
And whiche þei were & of whate degre
And eke in whatte arraie þat þei were inne
And att a knyghte þan wold I furst begynne

But secular love is the variety most interesting to the pilgrims. Their stories about it range from the bawdy jokes of the Miller's and Reeve's tales to the portrait of the ideally obedient wife, patient Griselda, of whom the idealistic Clerk tells us. One of the best stories comes from that most appropriate storyteller the Wife of Bath, the survivor of five husbands "and other company in her youth," an ardent pilgrim, and a woman who knows the "remedies of love" as well as Ovid. It takes the Wife a while to get to her story—a marvelous while, as she chatters on about the Church's irritating preference for virgins:

> A great perfection is virginity—
> And continence as well, and piety—
> But Christ, who of perfection is the well,
> Never commanded everyone to sell
> All that he had and give it to the poor
> And follow Him and his teachings evermore.
> He spoke to those who wished to live perfectly,
> And by your leave, good people, that's not me.

Even then she is not ready to begin her story; first we must hear about those five husbands and how she gained control over each. Each was a struggle. Four of them were obviously unworthy of her, and the

The art of manuscript illumination in both secular and religious books flourished during the medieval period. The beauties of this form lie in its use of rich color and splendid design, both evident in the prologue (left) from a fourteenth-century edition of the Canterbury Tales. *The miniature below, which shows a group of pilgrims on a journey to Canterbury, accompanied a sixteenth-century version of* The Story of Thebes *by John Lydgate, a poet whose reputation once rivaled Chaucer's.*

fifth and best is dead. It seems a sad life, and yet she is so energetic and tough-minded that she breaks off in the middle to express one of the finest acceptances of life in all literature:

> Lord Christ! when I recall
> My youth and my jollity and all,
> It tickles my heart's root and makes me gay.
> It does my heart good to this very day
> That I have had my world and in my time.
> But Age, alas, that poisons all our prime,
> Has reft me of my beauty and my pith—
> Let it go, farewell, the devil go therewith!
> The flour is gone, there is no more to tell;
> The bran, as best I can, now must I sell.
> But still to be right merry will I try.

And off she goes, without a tear, to tell about her fourth and fifth husbands. She is a grand woman, given to talking, it's true—"This is a long preamble of a tale," the Friar laughs—but her talk is well worth hearing. And the story she finally tells is one every woman should know.

It takes place in the days of King Arthur, when England was filled with fairies. But it is no simple romance, for scarcely have we met its hero, one of Arthur's knights, when he rapes a woman. Arthur sentences this miscreant to death, but the women at court intercede for him, and Queen Guinevere says she will pardon him if in a year and a day he can tell her what women most desire. The knight is pessimistic about his chances, and the Wife makes it clear that he should be when she rattles off a long list of reasonable guesses. After almost a year of fruitless search, the knight is heading gloomily homeward when he is stopped by an ugly old woman who offers him the answer if he will do what she asks. He agrees, she whispers it to him, and off they go to the court, where the knight tells Guinevere and her ladies:

> "My liege lady," said he, "generally
> Women desire to have sovereignty
> Over both their husband and their love,
> And to be in mastery them above."

He is right, he is pardoned, and now he must pay the old hag. Marry me, she says. And he does, but most ungraciously, sighing and muttering about his bad luck and her ugliness and age and lack of class. The old woman lectures him sharply and then gives him a choice: she will be ugly and faithful, or lovely and . . . and he must take his chances. The decision is too difficult for the knight and he gives up. "Choose for yourself," he says, thereby learning the lesson he had passed thoughtlessly on to the queen. Delighted, his wife promises to be both fair and faithful, and she turns herself into a beautiful young woman. The story's moral is obviously appropriate for the Wife of Bath, and it makes good psychological sense too: if we surrender ourselves to what we love, it will seem beautiful to us, whatever the world may see.

Dante warned us to love only the worthiest objects. The pale, sexless, loveless Pardoner takes as his text "the love of money is the root of

Apart from the beauty of its language, the enduring quality of the Canterbury Tales *stems from the rich variety of human types Chaucer created for it. Each of his twenty-nine characters seems embued with an unerring sense of the triumphs and foibles of human nature, and this makes their stories instructive as well as entertaining. A trio of these lively characters is shown above. From left to right: the Wife of Bath, the Miller, and the Pardoner. The stylized print at right, published in the Wynkyn de Worde chronicle of England in 1497, depicts London as it appeared in Chaucer's time.*

all evil," and that love, that self-centered greed, becomes the motivating force of a remarkable story. Its beginning almost puts us off, as the Pardoner launches into a conventional, example-laden sermon against drunkenness (about which he is suspiciously knowledgeable). But then he takes up the story of the three drunken rioters who see a friend's corpse carried by their tavern and hear the familiar religious exhortation *memento mori,* remember that you must die. In their drunkenness they decide "we will slay this false traitor Death," and off they stagger, cursing as they go. They soon meet another death-seeker, an old man who cannot die:

> Not even Death will take my life, alas,
> And like a restless captive I must pass,
> And on the ground, which is my mother's gate,
> I knock with my old staff both early and late,
> And say, "My dearest mother, let me in!
> Lo, how I vanish, flesh and blood and skin;
> Alas! when shall my old bones be at rest?"

An apparition weird enough to sober anyone, one might think, but the three rioters hear only the word *death,* and they insist that the old man reveal its whereabouts. He sends them to an oak tree under which they find a treasure hoard of florins. The action then moves swiftly through a ritual of double betrayal, a plot that writers have used and reused ever since, as the three are distracted from their pursuit of death by their greed, and then find death after all.

And to this tale Chaucer adds the amazing epilogue in which the arrogant Pardoner, having warned his fellow pilgrims well, out of gall or greed tries to sell them his fake relics! Chaucer told many fine stories in *The Canterbury Tales, Troilus and Criseyde,* and elsewhere, but never another so disturbing and so skillfully constructed.

Chaucer was an Englishman, of course, a native of London. The dialects used in such contemporary poems as *Piers Plowman* and *Gawain and the Green Knight* are now almost unreadable, but Chaucer's English is still generally intelligible. We must not draw the wrong conclusion, however. Chaucer's frenchified and latinate English survived because London has remained the political and economic center of Britain, but his style—urbane, secular, tolerant, and genially comic —is more representative of the Continent than of his own country. In his spirit Chaucer is one of the last international poets, and not typically British at all.

By Chaucer's time the native poetic tradition had already produced many fine Old English and Anglo-Saxon poems, notably *Beowulf*, *The Wanderer* and *The Seafarer*, and the now-fragmentary *Battle of Maldon*. That tradition preserved many Scandinavian elements as well as a sober Christian sense of mortality, and those great poems tend to dwell on the darker side of things. Dante had surveyed life religiously from the hereafter, and in the fourteenth century William Langland's

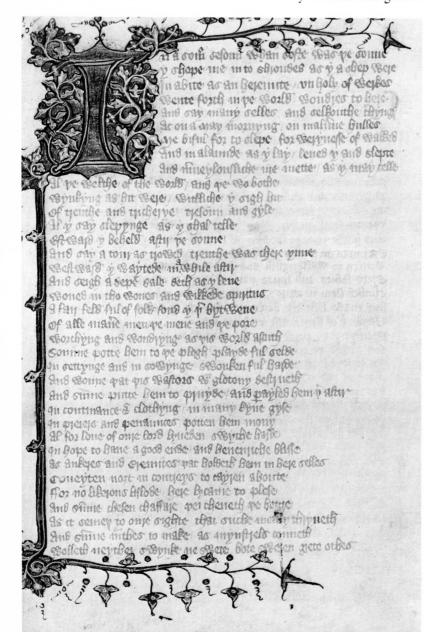

While Chaucer enlarged the scope of English poetry by incorporating French and Italian rhyme schemes into English, important poems were still being written in the alliterative verse style of Old English poetry. Among the very finest of these poems is the witty and trenchant social satire Piers Plowman *(early fifteenth-century manuscript shown at left), which is thought to have been written by William Langland. One of the most engaging figures in his Arthurian cast of characters is the golden-haired adventurer Sir Gawain, shown opposite with his lion-crested shield.*

long, three-version *Piers Plowman* made a comparable survey of England's "fair field full of folk." Not surprisingly, he found the field fairer than many of its folk. Even more than Chaucer, Langland criticized the clergy, and so angrily did he scold them that he was quoted by religious reformers even as late as the Reformation:

> Pilgrims and palmers   pooled together
> To seek Saint James   and saints at Rome;
> Went forth on their way   with many wise tales
> And had leave to lie   all their lifetime.
> Hermits in a heap   with hooked staves
> Went to Walsingham   and their wenches after them.
> Great lubbers and long,   that were loath to work,
> Clothed themselves in copes,   to be called brethren;
> And some shaped themselves as hermits   to have their ease.
> I found there friars   of all the four orders,
> Preaching to the people   for their bellies' profit . . .

Among these many Middle English surveys of life there appears one poem that concentrates on the testing and tempting of a single man, that treats him as heroic but fallible, and that shapes its story in a complicated verse form with exuberantly skillful artistry, with wit and high seriousness, with piety and courtliness, with clear-eyed realism and imaginative fantasy. The author, a contemporary of Langland and Chaucer, is unknown; the poem is *Gawain and the Green Knight*. In its subject and style it sums up the idealized chivalry that was already as far from contemporary English life as the heroic Greek world had been from Homer.

The scene is King Arthur's England—not as the Wife of Bath imagined it, with coarsely predatory knights and practical witches, but in all the gorgeous trappings of chivalric romance. On New Year's Day, a huge green knight on a green horse rides into Arthur's hall and challenges anyone there to cut off his head with the enormous ax he carries. The green knight's sole condition is that in a year and a day the beheader seek out the beheaded and offer up his own head. The reaction—or lack of it—is embarrassing: for a while it looks as though the king himself will have to accept the challenge. But then Sir Gawain begs that he be allowed to take Arthur's place, picks up the ax, and severs the monster's head. Unfazed, the green giant picks up his head —which then reminds Gawain of his promise—and monster and head ride off . . . to be sought by Gawain throughout a year of trials.

It is almost Christmas of the next winter when Gawain reaches a fine castle owned by a great gentleman and his beautiful wife. They entertain him very well—too well, in fact, for every day the husband goes out hunting, and every time he does the wife comes to Gawain's bedside and tries elegantly to seduce him. She fails; but when she hears about his forthcoming encounter with the giant, she persuades him to accept a magic sash and to conceal the gift from her husband.

On the appointed day Gawain presents himself at the giant's cave (from which issues the shrill sound of an ax being sharpened), and there he nervously bends his head to receive the blow. Twice he sees

the knight begin his swing, and twice he flinches slightly. Each time the knight stops and begins again, pointing out with some irritation that *he* hadn't flinched. (Yes, Gawain says, but if *my* head comes off, it will stay off.) On the third try Gawain holds still, but the ax merely cuts his skin. Then come the explanations: the green knight is actually the lord of the castle, and his beautiful wife is the enchantress Morgan le Fay. Gawain has been cut only because he has not been perfectly truthful; he has concealed the magic sash. Shaken and embarrassed by this revelation of his weakness, Gawain returns to Arthur's court wearing the sash conspicuously over his shoulder and confesses what has happened. The other knights cheer him up—obviously not understanding the seriousness of his adventure—and they decide that they will all wear similar sashes.

One can hardly praise too highly the richly detailed narrative, the delicate rituals of the castle and the hearty hunting scenes outside it, the giant's exuberant violence, and the elaborated courtesy of chivalric life framed by Gawain's journey through a cold English winter:

> When the cold clear water   was shed from the clouds
> And froze ere it could fall   to the pale fields,
> Near slain with sleet   he slept in his irons
> More nights than enough   in naked rocks
> Where clattering from the crest   the cold stream ran
> And hung high over his head   in hard icicles.

All these elements and more are put into the service of a sense of life and ethics too subtle and deep to be reduced to a moral or to a paraphrasable meaning. The poem is a fine farewell to a way of life that

The legend of Sir Gawain and the Green Knight is filled with the mystery, danger, and romance that were so pleasing to medieval audiences. In the illustration above, at left, the severed head of the Green Knight magically speaks to Sir Gawain, reminding him of their promised meeting in a year's time; above right, Gawain, having accepted Lord Bercilak's hospitality, tries to deflect the romantic advances of the lord's wife.

Europe has outlived, and its portrayal of Gawain not only as a heroic type but as a troubled and self-conscious individual anticipates some of the next major developments in Western poetry.

But we cannot leave this period without remembering the other side of life, the side that Chaucer touched with sunshine and good cheer in the bawdy tales of the Miller and the Reeve. Ordinary life is not always so light, nor were all poets so sophisticated as Chaucer or so piously good as Langland. Poetry came down to earth in the late Middle Ages, and nowhere more solidly—nor to dirtier earth—than in the thieves' jargon, the bleakly energetic outlook, the low-class subject matter, and the individual vividness of François Villon. Born poor in Paris in 1432 and raised by a chaplain whose name he adopted, Villon was a university graduate, a thief, a murderer, a jailbird, an offense to propriety, and an excellent poet. The refrain of his *Ballad of the Ladies of Former Times* is still known even in English: "Where are the snows of yesteryear?" But his poems, although often uneven and sometimes dubiously his, are valuable not merely because they provide tourist glimpses of that distant and dangerous world, but because they authentically evoke a sensibility as alive now as ever and seldom embodied in any art form.

Typical of his immediately personal style is one poem whose title tells the story: *Epitaph: in the form of a ballad that Villon made for himself & his companions, while waiting to be hanged with them.* The first and third stanzas give one a sense of his realism and his typical sinner's piety, and the grimly specific details contrast vividly with the polished generalities of the next century. In the lines that follow, the poet's fear of being mocked is based on his knowledge that at night playboys took their girls to the gibbets to see the hanged men. He had been there often enough himself:

> Human brothers, still living now we're stiff,
> don't be hardhearted whatever you do,
> but pity us poor clods, and if
> you do, God may sooner pity you.
> See us hang, 5 or 6 on show:
> as for the flesh, that greedy sot,
> it's left to be eaten itself, or rot;
> we bones to dust and ashes fall.
> Please, no one laugh at our sorry lot,
> but pray that God forgive us all.
>
> • • •
>
> The rain washes us and the sun dries;
> we're clean, but we blacken anyhow;
> magpies and ravens have gouged out our eyes
> and torn off every beard and brow.
> We never get to sit down now,
> but here or there, in the varying wind,
> at its pleasure constantly we spin,
> more pecked by birds than fruit on a wall.
> So don't make jokes at the mess we're in,
> but pray that God forgive us all.

Although greatly gifted as a poet, François Villon had an even greater talent for becoming embroiled in criminal activities. Twice he faced death by hanging for his crimes, but both times he received a reprieve. Following the second pardon, in 1463, Villon was banished from Paris and never heard from again. Fortunately, his poetic works were saved and published in 1489. The woodcut below, depicting a death by hanging, illustrated that edition.

4

In Praise of God, In Praise of Man

WITH THE DEVELOPMENT OF THE PRINTING PRESS in the sixteenth century, literature gained a new hold on immortality. But like most inventions, printing was a cause of trouble as well as delight. Thanks to it we possess many fine poems that would otherwise have been lost, but because of them poets bear a heavier burden, since so much poetry of the past endures to demonstrate what has already been thought, said, and achieved. Printing also increased the poet's sense of his own importance, all too often to the detriment of his anonymous universality. And while printing helped to save poetry from the inevitable errors of copyists, it also encouraged a kind of finicky polishing that sometimes has disastrous results.

Indeed, the whole notion of poetry as a polished, delicate, unwholesomely precious matter—a notion all too prevalent even today—developed during the sixteenth and seventeenth centuries, especially in France, where it almost crippled the form. We have seen that with the rise of nationalism and the Tower-of-Babel proliferation of literature in many languages, poetry developed more quickly in some areas than in others. With such medieval works as the *Song of Roland*, the *Romance of the Rose*, the Breton lays of Marie de France, and the ballads of Villon, the French seemed to have the beginnings of a vigorous if not a particularly profound national literature.

In the sixteenth century Pierre de Ronsard (1524–1585) and his fellow writers of the Pléiade group followed the precedent set by Dante two and a half centuries earlier and formally proclaimed that their native French was as acceptable for poetry as Latin. In itself this idea is harmless, or even good. But times had changed since the *Commedia* was written: the Pléiade did their work in a time of elegance and studious refinement, and instead of developing the strengths and energies of their language and its native poetic forms, they searched the classics for allusions, refinements, and high polish, which they imitated in their own poetry. The Pléiade also brought back obsolete, "poetic" French words, something Edmund Spenser was doing in England with similarly unsatisfactory results. Even worse, the French began the custom of rewriting Horace's casual precepts into binding rules. *The Art of Poetry*, they would call these revisions, but they seemed to make poetry a mechanical craft.

The Pléiade did produce some attractive poems—especially those

To escape the dangers of the dreaded plague that spread through London in 1665, John Milton moved his family to a country home, Chalfont St. Giles, in Buckinghamshire—and there he wrote his final works, Paradise Lost, Paradise Regained, *and* Samson Agonistes. *The house is now maintained as a museum, its study (opposite) filled with Milton memorabilia.*

Ronsard wrote "to Helen" in his more relaxed old age—but they also inaugurated several centuries of marbleized elegance and preciousness, centuries that have left behind them whole cities full of pillared ruins haunted by the pale ghosts of the Académie française. (The Académie was founded in the seventeenth century to carry on the Pléiade's work; one of its first accomplishments was the damning of Pierre Corneille's still-popular verse drama *The Cid* in 1638.) Not until the Romantic period would French poets attempt to write as freely and energetically as their fellow poets across the Channel, and even then Paul Verlaine would feel obliged to write his own *Art of Poetry* in which he followed the accepted rules of versification but suddenly shouted, "Take eloquence and wring its neck!"

But the benefits of printing were also great. The increasing wealth of available poems and the increasing numbers of people writing and reading knowledgeably all contributed greatly to the poets' understanding of verse. Art is artifice, and the artificer who does well must have a wide and deep knowledge of his profession. ("The life so short, the craft so long to learn," Chaucer had lamented.) Naïve simplicity can be pleasing, but simplicity alone quickly becomes merely simple. The Elizabethan-Jacobean period produced countless fine English poems, in part because poets had learned how not to be simple, how not to leave things out. Good poetry is never deliberately obscure, any more than good architecture is, or good mathematics. But just as the architect moves from the simplicity of a cave to the complexity of a mansion, and the mathematician rises from addition to logarithms, so the poet learns to express more and more of what he knows as he gains more awareness and control of structure, sound, imagery, argument, and ideas.

Sir Philip Sidney's long and complex sonnet sequence *Astrophel and Stella*, completed in 1591, begins with an especially artful sonnet in which he describes himself as having studied other poetry in hopes of learning how to praise his loved one:

> But words came halting forth, wanting invention's stay;
>   Invention, nature's child, fled step-dame Study's blows,
>   And others' feet still seemed but strangers in my way.
> Thus, great with child to speak, and helpless in my throes,
>   Biting my truant pen, beating myself for spite,
>   Fool, said my muse to me, look in thy heart and write.

We should not understand that last line too quickly. It seems to say that study, knowledge, and professional competence are useless to the poet —all he needs is some autobiographical, emotional impulse. But Sidney is not speaking personally; in fact he is studiously echoing Dante, who explained his "sweet new style" in the *Purgatorio* by saying:

> I am one who, when
> Love breathes in me, notes it, and in the same way
> that it spoke within me I go forth testifying.

Sidney, then, is not dismissing study; he is dismissing *mere* study in favor of professional knowledge that has been given life and intensity by personal feeling. Throughout our history poetry, like most of the

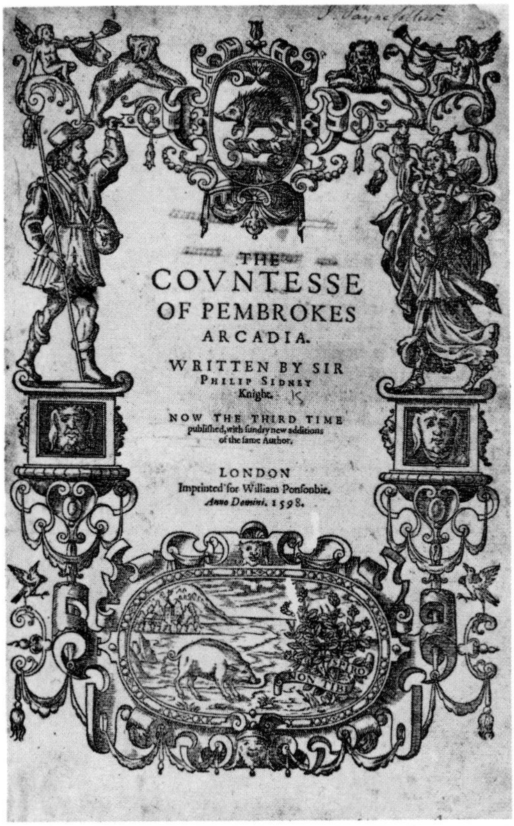

THE
COVNTESSE
OF PEMBROKES
ARCADIA.

WRITTEN BY SIR
PHILIP SIDNEY
Knight.

NOW THE THIRD TIME
publiſhed, with ſundry new additions
of the ſame Author.

LONDON
Imprinted for William Ponſonbie.
Anno Domini. 1598.

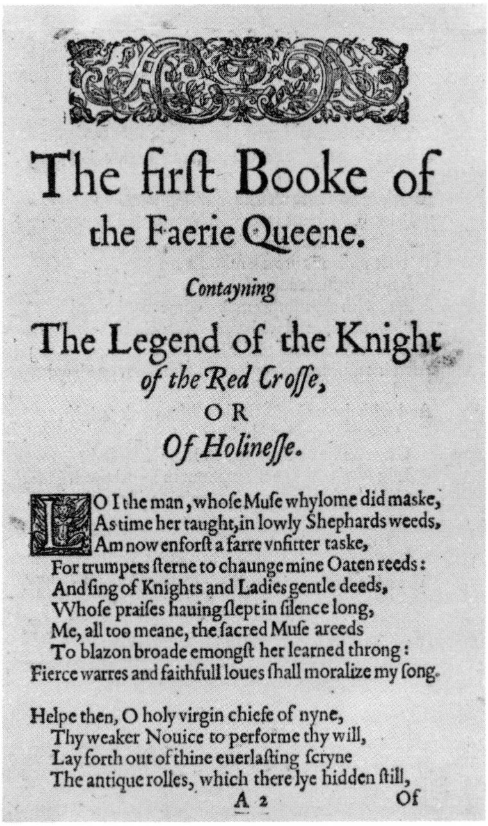

The firſt Booke of
the Faerie Queene.

Contayning

The Legend of the Knight
of the Red Croſſe,
OR
Of Holineſſe.

LO I the man, whoſe Muſe whylome did maske,
As time her taught, in lowly Shephards weeds,
Am now enforſt a farre vnfitter taske,
For trumpets ſterne to chaunge mine Oaten reeds:
And ſing of Knights and Ladies gentle deeds,
Whoſe praiſes hauing ſlept in ſilence long,
Me, all too meane, the ſacred Muſe areeds
To blazon broade emongſt her learned throng:
Fierce warres and faithfull loues ſhall moralize my ſong.

Helpe then, O holy virgin chiefe of nyne,
Thy weaker Nouice to performe thy will,
Lay forth out of thine euerlaſting ſcryne
The antique rolles, which there lye hidden ſtill,

A 2 Of

The invention of the printing press (detail above, left) facilitated the widespread dissemination not only of contemporary works but of the Greek and Roman classics as well. As the influence of the Renaissance reached outward from Italy, it found its finest poetic voice in France with the group of poets known as the Pléiade. The leader of this circle was Pierre Ronsard, shown in the engraving at left dressed in classic Greek garb. At the court of Elizabeth I a rebirth in English poetry was led by the consummate soldier-diplomat Sir Philip Sidney (title page of his poem Arcadia *above) and his contemporary Sir Edmund Spenser. In his epic work,* The Faerie Queene *(title page above, right), Spenser composed a paean to Elizabeth and her royal entourage phrased in a new and richly melodic rhyme scheme now known as the Spenserian stanza.*

arts, has vacillated between Apollo and Dionysus, thought and feeling, form and exuberance; but during this period poets were often extraordinarily, delightfully successful in getting the best of both worlds, producing vivid intensity even within the brief span of lyric poems.

It was a lucky thing, too, because a large and major poem became considerably less possible as the old certainties of Western culture cracked or collapsed. " 'Tis all in pieces, all coherence gone," lamented John Donne, and he spoke for many. That period of exuberant language, gay and costly clothing, expeditions to the far corners of the world, and wonderful poetry looks to us now like a marvelously vigorous time to be alive. But it was also a time when the struggles among national powers repeatedly threatened England's security, when the Catholic Church had been fragmented by the Reformation, when the meaningful, earth-centered, Ptolemaic universe was being replaced by the meaningless chaos of endless space, when explorers were reporting the existence of another hemisphere as big as the world previously known, when families were being broken up by political and religious controversies, and when Queen Elizabeth's childlessness threatened to plunge her country into civil war.

Scholars look coolly back on all this and speak calmly of "an age of transition." But every age is in transition; Augustan Rome and thirteenth-century Italy were changing as rapidly as Elizabethan England. The difference was that Vergil and Dante were able to see order in the change. There was no comparable understanding of life around 1600. The epics of Tasso, Camões, and Ariosto could find no persuasive order in existence, and Spenser's unfinished *Faerie Queen* breaks off after a long speech by Mutability, who argues that all earthly matters belong to her. The narrator is convinced, and the poem ends with him speaking of how he loathes life's instability and longs for the time

> when no more *Change* shall be,
> But stedfast rest of all things firmely stayd
> Upon the pillours of Eternity,
> That is contrayr to *Mutabilitie*:
> For, all that moveth, doth in *Change* delight:
> But thence-forth all shall rest eternally
> With Him that is the God of Sabbaoth hight:
> O that great Sabbaoth God, graunt me that Sabbaoths sight.

When poets of this age cast about for what might endure, the pessimists found nothing and even the optimists found stability not in life but only in art. "My verse your vertues rare shall eternize," Spenser tells his mistress. And Michael Drayton tells his:

> So shalt thou fly above the vulgar throng,
> Still to survive in my immortal song.

"He was not of an age, but for all time," Ben Jonson said of Shakespeare, and Shakespeare often said the same about his own poems:

Yet do thy worst, old Time: despite thy wrong
My love shall in my verse ever live young.

So long as men can breathe or eyes can see,
So long lives this, and this gives life to thee.

Not marble, nor the gilded monuments
Of princes shall outlive this powerful rhyme

Death to me subscribes,
Since spite of him I'll live in this poor rhyme
While he insults o'er dull and speechless tribes:
And thou in this shalt find thy monument
When tyrants' crests and tombs of brass are spent.

Seeking to unite an England torn by disputes over religion and the succession to the throne, Elizabeth I seized every opportunity to show herself to her subjects in the full panoply of her office—as can be seen in the picture at left in which the queen rides in a luxuriously appointed chariot. In 1576, John Shakespeare, a respected citizen of Stratford, applied for a coat of arms (drawing above)—the mark of a gentleman—for his family. Shakespeare's fortunes declined rather swiftly thereafter, however, and the application was denied. Twenty years later the suit was successfully reinstated by his son William.

Dante had seen in human and superhuman existence the complex patterns of the mystical numbers three and one, the unified relationship of good and evil, and God's complete control; he had only to imitate this order and control in his verse. But Shakespeare was far less convinced of God's providence, just as he was far less certain of the Tudors than Vergil was of the Caesars. As a result, his plays tend to be more coherent than their subject matter. *Othello*, for instance, is developed throughout with emphasis on two controlling images, blindness and poison. Othello cannot see Desdemona's faithfulness because Iago poisons his mind—and again and again the imagery drives this point home. There is a moral: we must see things as they are, however painful the process, or we risk having our vision poisoned. But the lesson goes unlearned, and at the end of the play, when the wedding bed is heaped with dead bodies because of Othello's blindness and Iago's poison, the dignitary from Venice who represents our fallible, mutable world is unable to face the facts. Gesturing toward the curtains of the bed, he tells a servant: "The object poisons sight; let it be hid." And the hidden poison is left to do more deadly work.

The same thing happens in *Hamlet*. The fateful inevitability of the action is repeatedly signaled in the play; willy-nilly, Hamlet must face conclusions. "The readiness is all." Yet the play's last words are left to that freelancing mercenary shark Fortinbras and to good old Horatio, whose conventional wisdom cannot accommodate itself to the disturbing events. Dying, Hamlet has asked Horatio to explain to the world what has happened:

If thou didst ever hold me in thy heart,
Absent thee from felicity a while,
And in this harsh world draw thy breath in pain
To tell my story.

But what can Horatio say? For him, too, all is in pieces, all coherence gone, and when he offers to explain "how these things came about" he can see only meaningless chaos:

So shall you hear
Of carnal, bloody, and unnatural acts,
Of accidental judgments, casual slaughters,

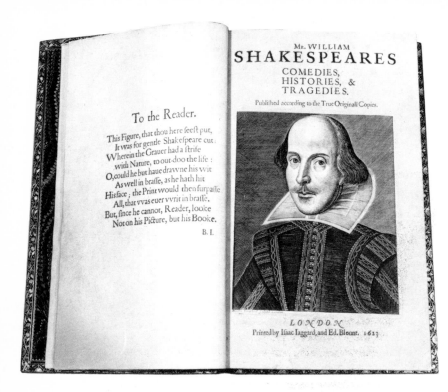

Of deaths put on by cunning and forc'd cause,
And in this upshot, purposes mistook
Fall'n on the inventors' heads: all this can I
Truly deliver.

"Truly" is a bit of Shakespeare's irony, but it is not the first warning of Horatio's inadequacy. Hamlet's dying words had conveyed the grim truth he had learned from the gravedigger and Yorick's skull: "the rest is silence." But Horatio had immediately blotted this out with conventional piety: "Good night, sweet prince," he replied, "And flights of angels sing thee to thy rest." He had missed the point, as usual; in the silence that is to come, no angels sing.

William Shakespeare (1564–1616), who usually spelled his name Shakspere, was the son of a Catholic merchant from Stratford-on-Avon in rural Warwickshire. He had only a grammar school education, if that—fellow poet Ben Jonson says he had little Latin and less Greek—and his first significant action was to marry Anne Hathaway, who was eight years older and several months pregnant. (With Susanna. Later she had twins, Judith and Hamnet.) An unpromising start, surely, and when he left his family to work in London as an actor of no great ability he probably confirmed the doubts of his Stratford neighbors.

Shakespeare was an ambitious man who disliked having to write plays for a living. In one of his sonnets he complains that Fortune

> did not better for my life provide
> Than public means which public manners breeds.
> Thence comes it that my name receives a brand,
> And almost thence my nature is subdued
> To what it works in, like the dyer's hand.
> Pity me then. . . .

Following his death in 1616, two actors from Shakespeare's original company undertook the task of gathering authentic copies of his plays for publication in a single volume. The job required both patience and diligence, for many of the original manuscripts had been lost or widely scattered. When the famed First Folio (left) was published in 1623, it included a portrait of the playwright by Martin Droeshout that is believed to have been approved by Shakespeare's widow, Anne, and is thus considered the only authentic likeness of him in existence. In 1609, an edition containing 154 of Shakespeare's sonnets had been printed, and the title page of that volume is seen at right.

He did prosper in his new profession, however: in 1596 he bought a large house in Stratford, and by 1610 he had retired there, writing a few last plays and some scenes for other men, and involving himself in several lawsuits. If he wrote it, as tradition says, his epitaph is the worst verse he ever wrote:

> Good frend for Iesus sake forbeare,
> to digg the dust encloased heare:
> Bleste be ye man yt spares thes stones,
> and curst be he yt moves my bones.

Once he had become commercially successful as an actor, writer, and shareholder in the Lord Chamberlain's Men, Shakespeare took no interest in publication. Those plays that were printed, like the sonnets, were printed by others, and the rest remained in manuscript and players' scripts until after his death. We know little about him, but everything we know suggests that the greatest poet the world has known had no "poetic" qualities at all, and that he would much rather not have written the plays that have made him more famed than Homer.

The young John Keats wrote a friend that "I am very near agreeing with Hazlitt that Shakespeare is enough for us," and it is certainly true that his works make up a world of words and people in which we can live very contentedly. Yet poets continued to write; and as the world changed, their poetry changed to fit it. John Donne (1573–1631) was born less than a decade after Shakespeare, but his life suggests some of the major changes that came about after Queen Elizabeth's death in 1603. Shakespeare spent his life writing, however reluctantly, for the theater. Donne began as a gentleman and a courtier who circulated his lyric poems in manuscript among his friends and who wrote in a complex and witty new style about the old and conventional topics—love, mistresses, death, and parting. Later, however, he was to grow pious, become a clergyman, write passionate religious poems and equally passionate sermons, and end his life as the dean of St. Paul's Cathedral.

As Donne turned, the world turned with him. That Scottish upstart King James had none of the glamour of Elizabeth, and earthly glory fell rapidly out of favor as the Puritans began preaching moral reform, emotional moderation, and imaginative dullness. Plays, poetry, and art all suffered as the general audience turned away from them. (And never turned back. It is commonly believed that poetry has moved away from ordinary people, but in fact the opposite happened.) Poets remained— the seventeenth century is rich and various in verse—but they found diminished audiences. Those with noble patrons wrote courtiers' verse; the others turned to piety, to simpler language, homespun imagery, and conventional religious ideas. Perhaps Donne's most representative successor was George Herbert, born in Wales in 1593 of noble parentage. (His mother, a pious and well-educated woman, had been a friend of Donne.) Herbert aspired for a time to a career in government before entering the church, but even during his years of secular ambition he wrote religious poetry exclusively. Those verses, published posthumously in 1633 as *The Temple*, include works of unusual metrical inventiveness. One such poem is *Easter Wings*:

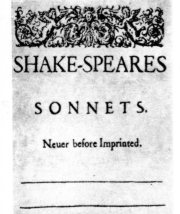

SHAKE-SPEARES

SONNETS.

Neuer before Imprinted.

AT LONDON
By *G. Eld* for *T. T.* and are
to be folde by *Iohn Wright,* dwelling
at Chrift Church gate.
1609.

Lord, who createdst man in wealth and store,
  Though foolishly he lost the same,
    Decaying more and more,
      Till he became
        Most poor:
        With thee
      O let me rise
    As larks, harmoniously,
  And sing this day thy victories:
Then shall the fall further the flight in me.

My tender age in sorrow did begin:
  And still with sicknesses and shame
    Thou didst so punish sin,
      That I became
        Most thin.
        With thee
      Let me combine,
    And feel this day thy victory:
  For, if I imp my wing on thine,
Affliction shall advance the flight in me.

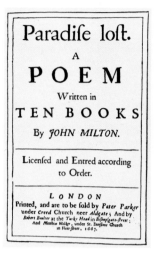

Herbert was an Anglican, while the dominant temper of England during the middle of the seventeenth century was, of course, Puritan. It is almost a paradox for such people to produce art of any sort, much less some of the greatest poetry in our language; but John Milton (1608–74) rose above his categories: he was more than a Puritan, more than a Christian, and decidedly more than his public role as Secretary of Foreign Tongues to the Council of State of the Puritan Commonwealth. In another sense, however, it might be said that all his poetry reflects that public role, since from early in his life he resolved not merely to be a great poet and "perhaps leave something so written to aftertimes, as they should not willingly let it die," but—like Vergil and Dante—to write with regard "to God's glory by the honour and instruction of my country." Although deeply read in Hebrew, Greek, and Italian literature and an excellent poet in what was still the international scholarly language, Latin, Milton decided to write his most impressive works in his "mother dialect" in order that "what the greatest and choicest wits of Athens, Rome, or modern Italy, and those Hebrews of old did for their country, I in my proportion with this over and above of being a Christian, might do for mine: not caring to be once named abroad, though perhaps I could attain to that, but content with these British Islands as my world. . . ."

Such confidence, expressed even before *Paradise Lost* was written, tends to put off ordinary people, as do the assurance, courage, and persistence with which Milton made himself into a great poet. Not even Vergil had been so deliberate in his self-creation; not even Dante had approached his high task with so little fear. And Milton was right. As he foresaw, the fame of *Paradise Lost* has been limited because of its being written in mere English, yet it is the greatest epic since the *Aeneid*, which it may even surpass. Indeed, it is one of the four finest

A clear-eyed, youthful stare, deepened by a belief in his own poetic genius, enlivens the portrait above of John Milton at the age of twenty-one. By the time he began to compose Paradise Lost *(title page above, left) some twenty-six years later, Milton's career as a public servant had been ended by changes in the political climate, and his artistic life had been hindered by encroaching blindness. Thus, it was against considerable odds that the poet set about his task, which was nothing less than to create a national epic. A page from Milton's original manuscript for* Paradise Lost *is seen above, at right. Although he distributed his poems among friends, George Herbert (engraving at left) did not attempt to publish them during his lifetime. However, a complete edition of his poems was issued posthumously in 1633.*

Paradise Lost.

To reign is worth ambition though in Hell:
Better to reign in Hell, than serve in Heaven.
But wherefore let we then our faithful friends,
Th' associates and copartners of our loss
Lie thus astonished on th' oblivious pool,
And call them not to share with us their part
In this unhappy mansion; or once more
With rallied arms to try what may be yet
270 Regained in Heaven, or what more lost in Hell?
So Satan spake, and him Beelzebub
Thus answered. Leader of those armies bright,
Which but th' Omnipotent none could have foiled,
If once they hear that voice, their liveliest pledge
Of hope in fears and dangers, heard so oft
In worst extremes, and on the perilous edge
Of battle when it raged, in all assaults
Their surest signal, they will soon resume
New courage and revive, though now they lie
280 Groveling and prostrate on yon lake of fire,
As we erewhile, astounded and amazed,
No wonder, fall'n such a pernicious height.
He scarce had ceased when the superior fiend
Was moving toward the shore; his ponderous shield
Ethereal temper, massy, large and round,
Behind him cast; the broad circumference

epics of the Western world, and no poet—not even Goethe in *Faust*—has approached its achievement since. Readers of earlier times grew up with *Paradise Lost* as they did with the Bible, and they delighted in the almost tangible reality that Milton gave to Christian stories and theology. For readers of our own times, when the Bible is less studied, *Paradise Lost* provides their grandest and most complex experience of Christian doctrine.

We have seen the Elizabethan concern with mutability, the collapse of once-stable institutions, and the threat of coming chaos. That era marked the rise of English lyric poetry, and the seventeenth century continued to produce many beautiful lyrics. But lyrics do not pretend to deal with the great issues of life or to take us deeply into truth; at most they provide what Robert Frost was to call "a momentary stay against confusion." Yet into this time of doubt and uncertainty Milton introduced the most assured voice in poetry, speaking about the most serious issues of life:

> Of man's first disobedience, and the fruit
> Of that forbidden tree whose mortal taste
> Brought death into the world, and all our woe,
> With loss of Eden, till one greater Man
> Restore us, and regain the blissful seat,
> Sing, heavenly Muse. . .
> That, to the height of this great argument,
> I may assert Eternal Providence
> And justify the ways of God to men.

It is a solemnly magnificent beginning, and the poem that follows is matched only by Dante's *Commedia* in its scope and depth of insight. The two poems are quite different, however. The *Commedia* is full of brilliantly conceived little scenes, but they are incidental to its general movement from Hell to Heaven. *Paradise Lost* is an epic drama, however, and one of its themes is the humanizing of humanity. When we first encounter Adam and Eve in the Garden of Eden they are gloriously and superhumanly perfect:

> Two of far nobler shape erect and tall,
> Godlike erect, with native Honour clad
> In naked Majesty seemed Lords of all,
> And worthy seemed, for in their looks Divine
> The image of their glorious Maker shone,
> Truth, Wisdom, Sanctitude severe and pure. . .
> For contemplation he and valour formed,
> For softness she and sweet attractive Grace,
> He for God only, she for God in him.

But such perfection does not endure, and where Dante's tone rises as he rises toward the heavens, Milton's progress is less happy:

> No more of talk where God or Angel Guest
> With Man, as with his Friend, familiar used
> To sit indulgent, and with him partake
> Rural repast, permitting him the while
> Venial discourse unblamed; I must now change
> Those Notes to Tragic; foul distrust, and breach
> Disloyal on the part of Man, revolt,
> And disobedience: On the part of Heaven
> Now alienated, distance and distaste,
> Anger and just rebuke, and judgment given,
> That brought into this World a world of woe. . . .

And so the tone must change from sublime and celebratory to grim and tragic. Yet that is not the end, thanks to God's grace and mercy, and Milton is able to leave his heroes and end his poem with simple language. He speaks of a sadly hopeful future for fallen humanity, even while Adam and Eve are being driven from their lost Paradise:

> They looking back, all the Eastern side beheld
> Of Paradise, so late their happy seat,
> Waved over by that flaming Brand, the Gate
> With dreadful Faces thronged and fiery Arms:
> Some natural tears they dropped, but wiped them soon;
> The World was all before them, where to choose
> Their place of rest, and Providence their guide:
> They hand in hand with wandering steps and slow,
> Through Eden took their solitary way.

But it is no safe or happy world they go into, nor will it ever be. Sobered by the failure of the Puritan cause and the return of a dissolute monarchy, Milton envisions a world of sorrow for mankind:

Truth shall retire
Bestuck with slanderous darts, and works of Faith
Rarely be found: so shall the World go on,
To good malignant, to bad men benign,
Under her own weight groaning, till the day
Appear of respiration to the just,
And vengeance to the wicked. . . .

One of Milton's most striking concepts, in his recreation of the story of Adam and Eve, is his heroic and apparently noble characterization of Satan. Although in his later appearances he is vile in shape and speech, Satan is introduced in such grand terms that many readers find him the true hero of the poem. He is not, of course, but the idea is tempting; Satan himself is tempting, and he is meant to be. Milton has a clear understanding of evil, and no conventional devil, no grotesquely comic red man with horns, tail, and cloven hoofs, could convey his awareness of the seductiveness of evil and the horror of good perverted. Satan was once the greatest of the angels, the closest to God of all created beings; that such goodness should be corrupted is a theme for tragedy, and Milton's Satan is fit to play the part.

As for the strength of evil's temptation, Milton was not willing to underestimate it; in a world "to good malignant, to bad men benign," we must prove our goodness continually, and we cannot do this ignorantly. We must know what evil is. "What wisdom can there be to choose, what continence to forbear without the knowledge of evil?" he asks in *Areopagitica*, his great essay against censorship. "I cannot praise a fugitive and cloistered virtue, unexercised and unbreathed, that never sallies out and sees her adversary, but slinks out of the race, where that immortal garland is to be run for, not without dust and heat."

Satan is therefore given many greatly daring actions and grand speeches, such as the one he makes on finding himself fallen into Hell:

> Farewell happy Fields
> Where Joy for ever dwells: Hail horrors, hail
> Infernal world, and thou profoundest Hell
> Receive thy new Possessor: One who brings
> A mind not to be changed by Place or Time.
> The mind is its own place, and in itself
> Can make a Heaven of Hell, a Hell of Heaven.
>   . . . Here at least
> We shall be free; the Almighty hath not built
> Here for his envy, will not drive us hence:
> Here we may reign secure, and in my choice
> To reign is worth ambition though in Hell:
> Better to reign in Hell, than serve in Heaven.

The rhetoric is gorgeous, but the content is a pack of lies, for Satan is like those sinners in Dante's Inferno, continuously recommitting their sins and redamning themselves. The mind *is* its own place, and Satan has made his into Hell. If we are attracted by his speeches, then Milton has made us feel the power of evil; Satan's actions and his fate should then be enough to enlist us among the good.

Himself a fallen rebel watched suspiciously by the newly restored monarchy, Milton completed *Paradise Lost*

> with mortal voice, unchanged
> To hoarse or mute, though fallen on evil days,
> On evil days though fallen, and evil tongues;
> In darkness, and with dangers compassed round,
> And solitude. . . .

Seventy years later the world had changed again, the debauched court of Charles II had given way to the dull domesticity of William and Mary, and man's sense of his relationship to God had altered too. A quite different man with a quite different voice now undertook to do Milton's work over again. Addressing himself to his friend and patron and using the casual tones of a witty gentleman, Alexander Pope (1688–1734) begins his *Essay on Man* with an echo of Milton:

> Awake, my St. John! leave all meaner things
> To low ambition, and the pride of kings.
> Let us (since life can little more supply
> Than just to look about us and to die)
> Expatiate free o'er all this scene of man;
> A mighty maze! but not without a plan. . .
> Laugh where we must, be candid where we can;
> But vindicate the ways of God to man.

Although known as one of the wittiest men of his age, Alexander Pope (portrait above by Michael Dahl) was also capable of serious writing. His poem An Essay on Man *(title page above, right), for instance, presents a rationale for the neoclassical view of society that he and his noted contemporaries Jonathan Swift and Thomas Parnell espoused.*

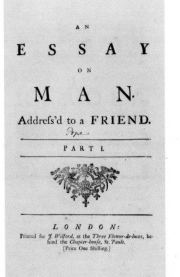

As the title suggests, Pope's chosen form is the versified essay, where heroic couplets serve excellently to convey the ordered, controlled, and eminently reasonable tone of his argument. His conclusions are equally cool: they involve no deep concern with sin; they say nothing of God's anger or of Hell; and they picture the world not as a place of suffering but as a fine place, whole, good, and cosmic in its order:

> All Nature is but art, unknown to thee;
> All chance, direction, which thou canst not see:
> All discord, harmony not understood:
> All partial evil, universal good:
> And, spite of pride, in erring reason's spite,
> One truth is clear: Whatever IS, is RIGHT.

However complex in grammar, diction, and allusions Milton's poetry might be, he still thought of poetry as essentially "simple, sensuous and passionate." Pope and his fellow poets of the eighteenth century, both in England and on the Continent, had a different sense of the matter. They followed the lead of the French in making poetry a rational art controlled by rules. (One of Pope's earliest poems was his *Essay on Criticism*, which served the century as an English *Art of Poetry*.) These poets wrote for a social audience delighting in wit, judgment, reason, common sense, and propriety; and they strove to imitate the classics. "Learn hence for ancient rules a just esteem," Pope wrote: "To copy nature is to copy them."

> True wit is nature to advantage dressed,
> What oft was thought, but ne'er so well expressed.

The engravings below, completed under Pope's supervision, adorned the frontispiece and a page in the first canto of the original edition of The Rape of the Lock, *published in 1714.*

Writing based on such rules has given our language a large stock of phrases, and for good reason. It "gives us back the image of our mind," aiming not at extraordinary depth or at individual insight, but at the polished expression of ideas with which we all agree. "A little learning is a dangerous thing"; "charms strike the sight, but merit wins the soul"; "fools rush in where angels fear to tread"; "who breaks a butterfly upon a wheel?"; "the feast of reason and the flow of soul"; "hope springs eternal in the human breast"—such passages suggest that dominant quality of eighteenth-century verse: art in the service of ideas, art as the maintenance of social order. It was not until the Romantic revolution that poetry could achieve tones other than those of reason, indignation, or satiric scorn. Once freed, the Romantic poets would look back scornfully on these eighteenth-century craftsmen. Keats would accuse them of having been

> closely wed
> To musty laws lined out with wretched rule
> And compass vile: so that ye taught a school
> Of dolts to smooth, inlay, and clip, and fit . . .
>
> .   .   .   .   .
>
> . . . with a puling infant's force
> They sway'd about upon a rocking horse,
> And thought it Pegasus.

5

The Romantic Revolution

THERE IS NO NECESSARY CORRELATION between a poet's greatest works and the end of his life. Shakespeare outlived his best plays by many years, and Pope wrote his best poems while still far from death. Wordsworth, most noticeably, lived on for almost half a century after his period of greatness, and Arthur Rimbaud abandoned poetry almost two decades before his early death. Yet we generally attach a specially high value to those works written by an author about to pass over into the great dark or the great light beyond.

When an author on the edge of this abyss looks back and condemns his work, we are unsettled. Vergil asked that the *Aeneid* be burned, and Chaucer condemned *The Canterbury Tales* as "worldly vanitees." This is troubling, as are John Keats' *Lamia* and his unfinished *Fall of Hyperion*, both of which suggest that if the poet had lived he would have qualified or denied most of the wisdom his poetry contains. On the other hand, poets who die after completing some admirable work seem thereby to give that work a special intensity and significance. Dante's *Paradiso* was found in his study, completed, after his death—as if, having described his visit to the highest bliss, the poet could not wait to return. In Shakespeare's *The Tempest*, the magician Prospero retires from his craft—"but this rough magic I here abjure"—and in his turning toward retirement, where "every third thought shall be my grave," we think we hear Shakespeare's own bittersweet farewell to the power of his pen and to the worlds it has created:

As a boy William Wordsworth explored thoroughly his native Lake District in northern England. Among his favored spots was an area of Westmorland known as Grasmere, about which he wrote "what happy fortune were it here to live." This ambition was fulfilled in December, 1799, when Wordsworth and his sister Dorothy moved into Dove Cottage (opposite), a charming country house that has become a symbol of the poet's life and work.

> Our revels now are ended. These our actors
> (As I foretold you) were all spirits, and
> Are melted into air, into thin air,
> And like the baseless fabric of this vision,
> The cloud-capp'd tow'rs, the gorgeous palaces,
> The solemn temples, the great globe itself,
> Yea, all which it inherit, shall dissolve,
> And like this insubstantial pageant faded,
> Leave not a rack behind. We are such stuff
> As dreams are made on; and our little life
> Is rounded with a sleep.

Mutability seems his final message, a mutability ended only by the sleep of the grave. Shakespeare's great successor as a poet-playwright,

John Dryden, was given a benefit performance in 1700, the last year of his life, and for it he wrote a brief *Secular Masque*. The poet and the century were ending their existence together; its heyday and his had been the sensual, exuberant reign of Charles II, a reign whose sinful memory now lay buried under middle-class propriety. The masque seems totally artificial: its characters are Momus, god of mirth, Diana, goddess of chastity and the hunt, Chronos, god of time, and Mars and Venus. Yet when, at the masque's end, they all sing together, we suddenly feel that Dryden has used his last genius to sum up and dismiss the whole brilliant and disappointing time:

> All, all of a piece throughout;
> Thy chase had a beast in view;
> Thy wars brought nothing about;
> Thy lovers were all untrue.
> 'Tis well an old age is out,
> And time to begin a new.

An artist's final view of life is likely to be pessimistic, or at least resigned. But the new intensity that produced Europe's several Romantic revolutions in art brought with them a new optimism, and it is especially strong in that great work of an entire artistic lifetime, Johann Wolfgang von Goethe's *Faust*. Goethe (1749–1832) wrote his earliest drafts of *Faust* before 1775, published the first half of the poem in 1808, and completed the work in 1831, sealing the manuscript and setting it aside for posthumous publication only eight months before his death. *Faust* therefore constitutes the epitome of his life's work and thought. Its intrinsic merits are easily enough understood to deserve our serious attention, but it gains further importance from its status as a kind of last testament.

The Faust legend is of central importance for this period. It recalls the Christian story of Satan's pride and fall, but it stems specifically from rumors that collected around the obscure German necromancer George Faust in the early sixteenth century. Those rumors, collected in a "Faust Book" after his death, later came to the attention of the Elizabethan poet-playwright Christopher Marlowe. Intrigued by power and its relationship with evil, Marlowe wrote a play that we possess only in garbled form but that serves even so to make a grand and mythical character out of the old German fraud. Marlowe's Doctor Faustus is a learned man who has seen through all legitimate knowledge. Expert in rhetoric, medicine, law, and divinity, he seeks greater power than they can offer him, and he sells his soul to the devil for that power. The result is a turmoil of activities, of which the most memorable is his calling up the spirit of Helen of Troy. Faustus greets her with a burst of praise that is like an aria:

> Was this the face that launched a thousand ships,
> And burnt the topless towers of Ilium?
> Sweet Helen, make me immortal with a kiss:
> Her lips suck forth my soul, see where it flies.
> Come, Helen, come, give me my soul again.
> Here will I dwell, for heaven is in these lips,

And all is dross that is not Helena.
I will be Paris, and for love of thee
Instead of Troy shall Wittenberg be sacked,
And I will combat with weak Menelaus,
And wear thy colours on my plumèd crest.
Yea, I will wound Achilles in the heel,
And then return to Helen for a kiss.
O, thou art fairer than the evening's air,
Clad in the beauty of a thousand stars.
Brighter art thou than flaming Jupiter,
When he appeared to hapless Semele:
More lovely than the monarch of the sky
In wanton Arethusa's azured arms,
And none but thou shalt be my paramour.

Such an achievement must be paid for, and Faustus' long speech as he waits for the devil to claim him is equally intense but painfully different in tone:

. . . The devil will come, and Faustus must be damned.
O I'll leap up to my God! Who pulls me down?
See, see where Christ's blood streams in the firmament!
One drop would save my soul, half a drop. Ah, my Christ!
Rend not my heart for naming of my Christ!
Yet will I call on him. O spare me, Lucifer!

Neither in Marlowe's *Doctor Faustus* nor in later versions of the story does Faust perform any great and heroic feats. His powers are

Sir Godfrey Kneller's portrait of the seventeenth-century poet John Dryden (left) reveals the grandeur of the man whose acute mind and stellar achievements in poetry, prose, and critical writings dictated the standards of his age. Johann Wolfgang von Goethe's journey through Italy in 1786 represented the fulfillment of a dream he had held since childhood. Accompanying Goethe on the trip was the artist Johann Tischbein, who painted the famous portrait of him entitled Goethe in der Compagna *(below, right). In addition to a journal he kept while traveling, Goethe completed many drawings of the Italian countryside. The view of the valley of San Pietro near Rome seen below is typical of Goethe's charming style.*

essentially inward, psychological; they originate in the amoral and even demonic urges deep inside us. The eighteenth century had attempted to repress or discipline such urges, even in its art; the Romantics attempted to use them fruitfully; and the decadents of later centuries would attempt to give way to these urges without being destroyed by them. But however one responds, the problem remains: whether put theologically or psychologically, whether embodied in Satan or Faust, power and aspiration are dangerous.

In Goethe's *Faust*, Faust's seduction of Gretchen and his attendance at the *Walpurgisnacht* orgies on the Blocksberg are evidence of these demonic urges, and Goethe is careful to avoid any suggestion of complete repentance or revulsion on Faust's part. If Faust is to be a complete man he cannot be a good man—this is one of the painful discoveries of the Romantic period. Wordsworth could describe the proper boundaries of man's activity by praising the skylark as "true to the kindred points of heaven and home," but Wordsworth felt no demonic urges; he was essentially domestic. For many Romantics, heaven and home were inadequate limits. Blake, for instance, would propose a *Marriage of Heaven and Hell*.

Faustus could not live happily ever after with Helen, nor Faust with Gretchen. It is a truth at once sad and comic that we can desire only what we do not possess. (For those who will not face this truth, modern advertising has prepared a hell in which desire is apparently satisfiable—if we will buy Brand X—only to be perpetually disappointed and renewed.) It was Goethe's Faust who first expressed this melancholy truth. Marlowe's Doctor Faustus had turned to magic for the satisfaction he could not find in permissible knowledge. Goethe's Faust knows better. He demands from Mephistopheles not satisfaction but desire—desire tantalizing, unachievable, thwarted, but always intense:

A drawing completed by Rembrandt many years earlier was the inspiration for the frontispiece (right) of an early edition of Goethe's Faust, The First Part of the Tragedy. *Although his renown made possible a life of the utmost luxuriousness, Goethe retained an uncomplicated life-style, as is evident in the painting below, which reveals the poet and his secretary working in a rather spartan study. The graceful watercolor at left illuminates a scene from one of Goethe's epic poems,* Hermann und Dorothea.

> Have you food that never gluts the appetite,
> Red gold restless for flight
> And slipping from the hand like mercury away,
> A game they never win who play,
> A girl who in my arms
> Already offers someone else her charms?
> . . . Show me ripe fruits that as they're picked decay,
> And trees whose leaves turn green again each day!

Faust has so thoroughly seen through mere satisfaction that he reserves his utmost contempt for the human who will settle for it:

> If ever I lie back, contented with inaction,
> Let me be ended quickly.
> If ever you with flattery can trick me
> Into smug complacency,
> If you can cheat me into satisfaction—
> Let that be judgment day for me!

What Faust demands of the devil is not satisfaction but action, not joy but experience, all the well-being and woe of human life. This is the insatiable hunger that Byron's life embodied for the Romantics, and it is a hunger for which life will always fail to provide sufficient food, strive as one may. More sadly, constant assertion of one's self, constant striving, will almost inevitably result in harm to other people (for the Romantics the chief evidence of this was the disastrous and death-strewn career of Napoleon), and if the striving hero possesses a moral code, the necessary result of his action is guilt.

Guilt was a feeling almost as foreign to Goethe as to Napoleon, however. Although by the end of Part I Faust has seduced and aban-

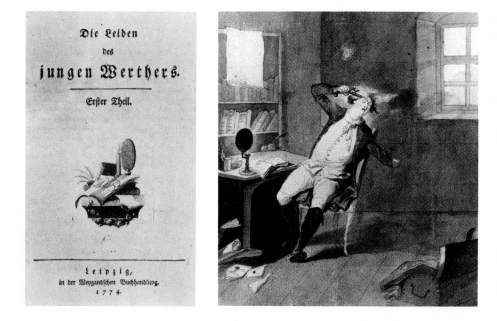

doned Gretchen and has been responsible for her death and that of three others, Goethe deals with the problem simplistically by sending to the sleeping Faust a spirit who erases both his guilt and his remembrance of evil actions. This allows him a comparatively pleasant striving through the rest of his life, and when he dies Goethe steps in once again and alters the traditional story. The devil is tricked, Faust escapes damnation, and a crowd of blessed women, including Gretchen herself, join in raising his soul to heaven. The Romantic period displayed some dizzying flights of optimism, but not even Shelley's *Prometheus Unbound* could imagine such a pinnacle of amoral blessedness for striving and sinful man.

Faust is an unsatisfactory work. Satisfaction would seem irrelevant in such a work, of course, even self-contradictory—but we need not assume that Goethe deliberately failed for the sake of his thesis. A rationally perfect work of art is conceivable only, within human limits, at the end of a period of development in art and thought. The *Aeneid* is built upon a mature epic tradition, for instance, and *Paradise Lost* works with that tradition plus sixteen centuries of Christianity. But in *Faust* Goethe deals with a comparatively unexplored myth (Thomas Mann's great twentieth-century novel *Doctor Faustus* shows how complex such themes can become), and he has no fixed literary form to use. He must feel his way emotionally, intuitively, and artistically into his story's possibilities and implications. It is no wonder, then, that the task required his intermittent attention throughout his life, and that the resulting work should contain more ideas than he was able to develop and resolve. Despite the mature Goethe's love for classical clarity and sharpness of definition, *Faust* is a wild drama acted in the dark, thundering stormily, lulling us with momentary calms, and lighted brilliantly but erratically by his flashes of imagination.

Meanwhile, equivalents of the Faust story were being developed in England. While *Faust* was slowly evolving in Germany, first Blake and then Byron and Shelley were imagining and versifying their own independent but similar stories of heroic aspiration, sin, struggle against

The Sorrows of Young Werther (*title page, above left*), published in 1774, marked the emergence of Goethe as a major figure in German letters. The author himself executed the watercolor above, which depicts the lovelorn Werther's suicide. Empathy with Goethe's tragic hero was so profound among romantic Germans that the work inspired a rash of similar suicides. In later, poetical works such as Faust, Goethe was specifically to reject the emotionalism of Werther. Goethe and the lyric poet Johann Christoph Friedrich von Schiller (*right, above*) enjoyed a particularly close professional association during the late 1700s, when the two were recognized as the foremost exponents of Weimar classicism. Heinrich Heine (*right, below*), a chief inheritor of the German romantic tradition, is remembered for his Book of Songs, which includes a famous ballad in which he created the myth of the Lorelei.

evil, and "mental fight." In its most hopeful form, this struggle is described in Blake's preface to his epic *Milton*:

> And did those feet in ancient time
> Walk upon England's mountains green?
> And was the holy Lamb of God
> On England's pleasant pastures seen?
>
> And did the Countenance Divine
> Shine forth upon our clouded hills?
> And was Jerusalem builded here
> Among these dark Satanic Mills?
>
> Bring me my Bow of burning gold:
> Bring me my Arrows of desire:
> Bring me my Spear: O clouds unfold!
> Bring me my Chariot of fire!
>
> I will not cease from Mental Fight,
> Nor shall my Sword sleep in my hand,
> Till we have built Jerusalem
> In England's green & pleasant Land.

William Blake (1757–1827) was as confirmed a Londoner as Chaucer, although he was no courtier but a fierce hater of kings, priests, and that judging, condemning, and repressive old God in the sky whom he sometimes called Nobodaddy. An eccentric engraver and poet who made and illustrated most of his own books, Blake was little known in his own time and often dismissed as a madman, but his delicately ambivalent *Songs of Innocence and Experience* and sprawling, prophetic poems are today the object of intense study, and their religion-hating author is the object of almost religious veneration.

Blake envisioned for mankind an energetic heaven, Jerusalem, to be inhabited by the giant Albion, who represents at once England, humanity, and each of us. Perhaps we were there before, in some early Eden, but now we have fallen into our present world of time and space, the grim world of society and Experience. Here our spiritual self is imprisoned in matter—in our bodies and our stony, hellish world—because of our mental submission to that jealous Nobodaddy and his kings and priests. This condition is the controlled, chartered, and bleak world summed up in Blake's *London*:

> I wander thro' each charter'd street,
> Near where the charter'd Thames does flow,
> And mark in every face I meet
> Marks of weakness, marks of woe.
>
> In every cry of every Man,
> In every Infant's cry of fear,
> In every voice, in every ban,
> The mind-forg'd manacles I hear.
>
> How the Chimney-sweeper's cry
> Every black'ning Church appalls;

And the hapless Soldier's sigh
Runs in blood down Palace walls.

But most thro' midnight streets I hear
How the youthful Harlot's curse
Blasts the new born Infant's tear,
And blights with plagues the Marriage hearse.

It is through "mental fight" that we may destroy this material prison, through an explosive release of our presently repressed or perverted instincts and passions. In the external world, the images of this fight include the American and French revolutions, both of which Blake celebrated in verse. But his most famous image is that awesome figure of imagination unfettered: the Tyger.

Blake's insistence upon overthrowing Nobodaddy and his burning desire to build Jerusalem in England's green and pleasant land were to be echoed by a poet who knew nothing of him—Percy Bysshe Shelley,

Perhaps the most famous lines Blake ever wrote —"Tyger, Tyger, burning bright / In the Forests of the night"—appear in the poem from Songs of Experience *entitled* The Tyger, *seen at far left with the author's original hand-colored illustration. Scotland's history, folk legends, and natural landscape provided the material from which both Sir Walter Scott (far right) and Robert Burns (near left) fashioned poems of narrative power and lyric beauty. Scott eventually concentrated his energies on the novel, but Burns found endless inspiration in the songs and language of Scotland. The original draft of Burns's* On hearing a thrush sing on a morning walk in January *is reproduced above.*

Ill health and fear of social harassment due to their unusual household—which included Lord Byron's mistress, Claire Clairmont, and her daughter Allegra—caused Percy Bysshe Shelley and his wife, Mary, to leave England for Italy in 1818. During the four years he spent in Italy Shelley composed such masterworks as Prometheus Unbound, The Cenci, and Epipsychidion. The English portraitist Joseph Severn captured the youthful Shelley in a delightfully romantic pose in the painting opposite, showing him seated in a ravine near the ruins of the Baths of Caracalla in Rome.

the delicate son of a wealthy country squire, born a third of a century after Blake and educated at Eton and, briefly, at Oxford. Shelley (1792–1822) spent much of his brief stay in the material world attempting to enlighten his fellowman, usually in vain. He was expelled from Oxford for his part in writing and printing an essay titled *The Necessity of Atheism*. He then befriended sixteen-year-old Harriet Westbrook. "Her father has persecuted her in a most horrible way," he wrote, "& endeavours to compel her to go to school." To save her from this fate worse than death, Shelley married her. His next project was to free Ireland. Marriage was out of the question in this case, so he wrote an *Address to the Irish People*, one that he succeeded in distributing around Dublin by tying copies to balloons and setting them free over the city.

Life went on like that. Eventually Shelley left England with another woman—Harriet later committed suicide—and he spent the rest of his short life in Europe. He died as he had often predicted he would, when his sailboat sank in a storm (after what may have been an attack by pirates). His body was washed ashore near Viareggio, and there his friends, including Byron, cremated it on the beach. His ashes were buried in the Protestant Cemetery in Rome, near the tomb of John Keats. It was in memory of Keats that Shelley had written one of his greatest poems, *Adonais*, in which he eloquently expressed his desire to escape this material world and to join Keats in eternity:

> The One remains, the many change and pass;
> Heaven's light forever shines, Earth's shadows fly;
> Life, like a dome of many-coloured glass,

Shelley and his close friend Edward Williams died in 1822 when a sudden storm sank the poet's boat as it sailed in the Gulf of Spezia. In the painting below, Lord Byron and his patron and companion Leigh Hunt observe the cremation of Shelley's body near the spot where it washed ashore at Viareggio. Lord Byron, seen in Albanian national dress in the portrait at right by Thomas Phillips, alternately shocked and stimulated Victorian England, which followed his romantic and literary exploits much as modern audiences might follow those of a popular movie star.

Stains the white radiance of Eternity,
Until Death tramples it to fragments.—Die,
If thou wouldst be with that which thou dost seek!

. . . . . .

The breath whose might I have invoked in song
Descends on me; my spirit's bark is driven,
Far from the shore, far from the trembling throng
Whose sails were never to the tempest given;
The massy earth and spherèd skies are riven!
I am borne darkly, fearfully, afar;
Whilst, burning through the inmost veil of heaven,
The soul of Adonais, like a star,
Beacons from the abode where the Eternal are.

Shelley's improbable friend George Gordon, Lord Byron (1788–1824), came of a family as strange as Shelley's was conventional. His mother's ancestors were obscurely wild—as was his dish-throwing mother herself—but Byron was more concerned with his father, "Mad Jack," who had abandoned his wife and children and who died when Byron was three; his grandfather, Admiral "Foulweather Jack," who

Scene 1st Act 1st
Manfred

The lamp must be replenished but even then
It will not burn so long as I must watch.
My slumbers – if I slumber – are no sleep
But a continuance of ~~constant~~ enduring thought
Which then ~~I cannot resist at~~ I can resist not – in my heart
There is a vigil – and these eyes but closed
To look ~~from~~ within, – and yet I live and bear
The aspect & the form of living men

Philosophy and ~~knowledge~~ science and the springs
Of wonder – and the wisdom of the world
I have essayed and in my mind there is
A power to make these subject to itself–
But they avail not; – I have done men good
And I have met with good even among men
But this avail'd not – I have had ~~my foes~~
And none have baffled – ~~and~~ many fallen before me
But this avail'd not – good or evil;
Powers – passions – all I see in other beings
Have been to me as rain upon the sands
Since that all nameless hour. I have no dread

94

Lord Byron's literary alter ego —the melancholy and driven Byronic hero—was introduced in the vivid poetic travelogue entitled Childe Harold's Pilgrimage *(near left) and then reappeared again and again in many dramatic poems, including the story of Lord Manfred (holograph, far left). Although Byron was short, clubfooted, and inclined toward plumpness, the romantic aura that surrounded him assured the poet a constant stream of female companions—as the caricature at left, below, indicates. Living in Russia and isolated from current literary movements in Europe, Aleksandr Pushkin (portrait above) developed a poetic style well suited to what he called the "roughness and simplicity" of the Russian language.*

seemed to attract storms; and his granduncle William, "the Wicked Lord," who had killed a neighbor in a duel. Raised in Calvinist Scotland, the boy Byron soon identified himself with Abel's brother and murderer, Cain. He was handsome and athletic but hindered by a clubfoot, which he seems to have suspected of being the devil's mark on him, and he dabbled in sin through homosexual liaisons and incest with his half-sister Augusta. After a desultory education at Cambridge (where, since dogs were forbidden, he kept a bear) he went on a splendidly romantic tour of the Near East, from which he returned with the first two cantos of *Childe Harold's Pilgrimage.*

Published in 1812, they caused great excitement; as Byron himself later said: "I awoke one morning and found myself famous." These two cantos and the two that followed by 1818 tell of an obscurely guilty and mournful young man who, as Matthew Arnold would describe him, bore through Europe "the pageant of his bleeding heart." Hundreds of sympathetic women rushed to comfort the author, presuming that he was sharing Childe Harold's distress, but Byron soon condemned himself to a foolish and short-lived marriage to Isabella Milbanke, the inappropriate woman he nicknamed "the Princess of Parallelograms." A year later, in 1816, he left England forever. His Faustian rise and collapse—for Byron, hell and marriage were equivalents—was accompanied by a flood of poems in which Byron struck appropriate poses:

> . . . I seek no sympathies, nor need;
> The thorns which I have reap'd are of the tree
> I planted: they have torn me, and I bleed:
> I should have known what fruit would spring from such a seed.

Like Faust, Byron found life painfully inadequate to his intense aspirations, although he turned not to the art of magic but to the magic of art:

> 'Tis to create, and in creating live
> A being more intense, that we endow
> With form our fancy, gaining as we give
> The life we image, even as I do now.

His verse-play *Manfred* expresses the quintessence of his Faustian drama, even though Byron knew little of Goethe's *Faust,* Part I, and nothing of Marlowe's *Doctor Faustus. Manfred* is a great, sinful nobleman with a castle in the Alps, burdened by a strange guilt and driven by demonic passions. Like Faustus, he knows that he is damned, but he will acknowledge no external power. When devils come for him he drives them off, echoing Milton's Satan as he does:

> The mind which is immortal makes itself
> Requital for its good or evil thoughts,—
> Is its own origin of ill and end—
> And its own place and time . . .
> *Thou* didst not tempt me, and thou couldst not tempt me;
> I have not been thy dupe, nor am thy prey—

95

But was my own destroyer, and will be
My own hereafter.—Back, yet baffled fiends!—
The hand of death is on me—but not yours!

In Germany, Goethe—who was to include a Byronic character in *Faust*, Part II—reviewed *Manfred*, saying in part that "this singular intellectual poet has taken my *Faust* to himself. . . . He has made use of the impelling principles in his own way, for his own purposes, so that no one of them remains the same; and it is particularly on this account that I cannot enough admire his genius."

There is another Byron entirely, the lively satirist and man of the world whose voice—in *Beppo*, *The Vision of Judgment*, and especially the marvelous *Don Juan*—was a model for Pushkin's *Eugene Onegin* and is now the principal delight of Byron's readers. But for the nineteenth century it was Byronic melancholy and Byronic guilt that

The London banker Samuel Rogers was a friend and patron of many English poets during the early nineteenth century. Charles Mottrams' engraving below shows Rogers hosting a breakfast party to which he invited Wordsworth (third from left, seated at table), Coleridge (fifth from left), and Byron (second from right). An accomplished man of letters, Coleridge (near right) is perhaps best remembered for his poetic adventure tale The Rime of the Ancient Mariner *(Gustave Doré engraving at far right).*

most enchanted the young readers of two continents and that was to flower darkly in Edgar Allen Poe and Charles Baudelaire.

Meanwhile, other poets found other images and tones—and sometimes other themes. Among the early Romantics, Samuel Taylor Coleridge (1772–1834) gave us the dreamy wish-fulfillment of *Kubla Khan*, the ominous fable-fragment *Christabel*, and the mythical adventures of *The Rime of the Ancient Mariner*. All three poems take us to romantic places long ago and far away, and yet they are not escapist literature. Indeed, both *Christabel* and the *Ancient Mariner* deal with sin and guilt—most obviously in the Mariner's shooting of the albatross and his endless attempts to expiate that offense—and the cold and isolated settings are as emblematic as those of Dante's *Commedia*. But the guilty Mariner has none of the arrogance and ambition of Dante's sinners or of Faust; Coleridge's characters are only miserable victims trapped in their consciences, as Coleridge himself had been trapped by an unhappy family life and frightened schooldays.

Like Byron, Coleridge had another side to his poetic character— a gently Wordsworthian meditative voice, one heard especially in the quiet musings of *This Lime-Tree Bower My Prison* and *Frost at Midnight*. In such poems he shows us the imagination's ability to use nature as the language of its feelings, seeing natural objects as the potential imagery that

> . . . the idling Spirit
> By its own moods interprets, everywhere
> Echo or mirror seeking of itself.

Coleridge left us many valuable poems, but he was only a part-time poet. His friend William Wordsworth (1770–1850) made poetry the primary activity of his life. With Byron, Wordsworth shared the attention of the nineteenth century, and as the longest-lived of the Romantics he stayed on to shape the Victorians' understanding of the Romantic inheritance. Wordsworth began life as a potential ne'er-do-well. He sponged off his relatives rather than going dutifully to work after college; he spent a lot of time in revolutionary France, sharing the liberals' hostility toward England; and he had an affair with a young French woman, who bore him a daughter. Only the accidents of political radicalism drove him from France and his potential future as an expatriate. Once back in England, however, he soon cooled down. His delightful sister Dorothy, who was to spend her life with him, introduced Wordsworth to the pleasures of nature, and his friend Coleridge taught him new theories of psychology and poetry. The result was not only a series of well-known poems about daffodils, cuckoos, and solitary reapers, but a number of long and deep meditations on our relationship with our past and with the material world.

No more than Blake, Coleridge, Shelley, or Byron did Wordsworth believe that we are essentially physical beings. Early in his career he stated his theme in magnificent lines that remind us of Blake even as they echo Milton:

> All strength—all terror, single or in bands,
> That ever was put forth in personal form—
> Jehovah—with his thunder, and the choir
> Of shouting Angels, and the empyreal thrones—
> I pass them unalarmed. Not Chaos, not
> The darkest pit of lowest Erebus,
> Nor aught of blinder vacancy, scooped out
> By help of dreams—can breed such fear and awe
> As fall upon us often when we look
> Into our Minds, into the Mind of Man—
> My haunt, and the main region of my song.

The relationship between the awesome Mind of Man and the external world was a constant problem for Wordsworth. In his hopeful youth and his conventional old age he thought of Nature as a source of wisdom and comfort; between these two periods, and while writing his finest poetry, he was deeply troubled by the disparity between Nature's cyclic vitality and Man's unstoppable sinking from childhood's glories into old age and death. The drowning of his favorite brother, John, in a stormy shipwreck gave the poet particular reason to turn bitterly against his early belief that "Nature never did betray the heart that loved her"; and in the fine passage that ends his spiritual autobiography, the *Prelude*, Wordsworth addresses Coleridge in terms that are almost Blakean in their dismissal of the natural world, for all its beauties:

> . . . what we have loved,
> Others will love, and we will teach them how;

Even in the brilliant company of Coleridge, Byron, Keats, and Shelley, the achievement of Wordsworth stands alone for its balanced combination of intellectual depth and beauty of language. The portrait above, drawn by Benjamin Haydon in 1818, is the first of several studies of the poet he undertook. In the photograph at right a grouping of some of the artifacts of Wordsworth's daily life is highlighted by a bunch of daffodils, the inspiration for one of his most delightful poems.

Instruct them how the mind of man becomes
A thousand times more beautiful than the earth
On which he dwells, above this frame of things. . .
In beauty exalted, as it is itself
Of quality and fabric more divine.

Most of Blake's early works had already been published when the period's latest—and one of its finest—poets was born. John Keats (1795–1821), the son of a well-to-do livery stable owner, lost both parents early in life, was cheated of most of his inheritance, studied to be a doctor, and then committed himself to the writing of poetry until his early death from the tuberculosis that had killed his mother and one brother. His poetic career covered less than four years, during which time he wrote dazzling poems, became one of the finest craftsmen poetry has known, and learned on his pulse most of the major ideas of his period.

As his wonderful letters demonstrate, Keats was an immensely intelligent, lively, funny, and likeable young man, eminently suited to enjoy the world. His poetry expresses and explores this enjoyment. Assuming as the other Romantics had done that the senses, emotions, and imagination—rather than cold reason—are the proper means, and that beauty is their end, Keats's poetry plunges into the world of intense experience. Using every device that verse can employ, Keats evokes the rise of imaginative and sensual intensity to that climax in which life seems justified.

If his poetry is a fine expression of this gusto, however, it is also a critique of it. By the end of his short career, in those magnificent poems *Ode to Psyche, Ode to a Nightingale, Ode on a Grecian Urn,* and *On Melancholy,* Keats at once evoked this pursuit of imaginative pleasure and showed us its limitations, its brevity, and finally its inadequacy. "Beauty is Truth, Truth Beauty," the Grecian urn tells us; "That is all ye know on earth, and all ye need to know." But the urn is wrong, even though it expresses an idea that Keats had once believed in. There are truths beyond beauty, he knows now, and beauties beyond our desiring. Goethe's Faust was right in seeing that this world alone could not satisfy us; Keats went further, and showed us that even intense desire is not enough. Much beyond this he had no time to go. Disappointed in his love for Fanny Brawne and in his hopes for his poetry, seriously ill and nearly impoverished, he set sail for Rome and a painfully drawn-out death. Before that time, however, he wrote one of his finest poems, that quiet and unsentimental acceptance of mortality, *To Autumn.*

Season of mists and mellow fruitfulness,
    Close bosom-friend of the maturing sun;
Conspiring with him how to load and bless
    With fruit the vines that round the thatch-eaves run;
To bend with apples the mossed cottage-trees,
    And fill all fruit with ripeness to the core:
      To swell the gourd, and plump the hazel shells
With a sweet kernel; to set budding more,
    And still more, later flowers for the bees,
    Until they think warm days will never cease,
      For Summer has o'er-brimmed their clammy cells.

Who hath not seen thee oft amid thy store?
    Sometimes whoever seeks abroad may find
Thee sitting careless on a granary floor,
    Thy hair soft-lifted by the winnowing wind;
Or on a half-reaped furrow sound asleep,
    Drowsed with the fume of poppies, while thy hook
      Spares the next swath and all its twinèd flowers:
And sometimes like a gleaner thou dost keep
    Steady thy laden head across a brook;
    Or by a cyder-press, with patient look,
      Thou watchest the last oozings hours by hours.

Where are the songs of Spring? Aye, where are they?
    Think not of them, thou hast thy music too,—
While barrèd clouds bloom the soft-dying day,
    And touch the stubble-plains with rosy hue;
Then in a wailful choir the small gnats mourn
    Among the river sallows, borne aloft
      Or sinking as the light wind lives or dies;
And full-grown lambs loud bleat from hilly bourn;
    Hedge-crickets sing; and now with treble soft
    The red-breast whistles from a garden-croft;
      And gathering swallows twitter in the skies.

6

Conservatism and Decadence

POETRY AFTER THE ROMANTIC PERIOD presents us with some strange and contradictory situations. In England, Alfred Tennyson published *In Memoriam* in 1850—and Prince Albert liked it so well that Queen Victoria made Tennyson her poet laureate. In France in the same decade, Charles Baudelaire published his *Flowers of Evil*—and the Paris police prosecuted him for an offense to public morality, fined him, and banned six of his poems. In England, the sweet heroine of Robert Browning's poetic drama *Pippa Passes* innocently misused (and mispronounced) a naughty four-letter word because her creator was too naïve to know what it meant; "a distinctive part of a nun's attire," he thought, and no one ever dared to enlighten him. But in France, Baudelaire and Arthur Rimbaud explored the depth of moral and physical degradation in their poetry, and in order to know their subject they plunged into perverse sensuality, intensive drug-taking, and radical alterations of the mind. "I say that one must be a *seer*, make oneself a *seer*," Rimbaud wrote. "The poet makes himself a *seer* by a long, immense, and irrational disordering of all the senses."

Down through the ages poetry had concerned itself with many great themes. Heroic action was Homer's, the greatness of the Roman state was Vergil's—and Dante rose even higher, describing man's relationship to God. After the Elizabethans had balanced earthly glory against the mutability of all things, Milton returned to Dante's theme, and even the less ambitious poets of the eighteenth century attempted to settle the standards of society. Then the Romantics went deeply into the mind: its relationships to society, the natural world, and its own past—and its vaulting and unfulfillable desires for power, knowledge, and love.

It was a great heritage, then, that awaited poets of the later nineteenth century, but it was accompanied by increasing difficulties. Not only in the subject matter of poetry and its styles—these have always been difficult, and great poets have always had to renew the past— but in the difficulty of finding an audience. The Puritans' revolt against art in the name of religion and morality had destroyed or alienated the homogeneous audience that, for most of Western history, had listened eagerly to its poets; and those readers who remained were not only fewer but tended to group into coteries and cliques. By the early eighteenth century many of these fragmentary audiences—those who supported religious poets or elegant lyricists, for instance—had almost disappeared, and even such poets as Pope, Prior, Gay, Johnson, Goldsmith, and Gray wrote only for the educated few. That audience basically employed its poets to speak for them, not to them; to versify "what oft was thought, but ne'er so well expressed."

Such an audience affects what the poet can say. We are almost always less sensitive, perceptive, and intelligent in a group than we are as separate individuals, and the poet who must satisfy a group's taste cannot develop all his personal powers. Yet he must satisfy his audience or starve. The Romantic period gave the poet some help in this regard, for the middle class was rising more quickly and successfully than ever before, was educating its children better, and was attempting to develop a taste in the arts. This relatively new audience did less dictating and more learning—and as a result the poet could teach his audience instead of merely mirroring it. Wordsworth especially took advantage of this opportunity. He insisted that he wrote for everybody, not merely for a coterie, and he defined the poet as nothing less than "a man speaking to men." Since the poet's new subject was the mind of man, and since we all have minds, what he had to say was of interest to everyone, and Wordsworth developed a clear style of writing intelligible to all.

But the mind of man is at once the most general of subjects and the most private. It can lead the poet to speak about all mankind, but it can also lead him into the most obscure and introspective of private investigations. He may discuss those central qualities of healthy minds that constitute every human's ideal self, but he may also go deeply into individual psychology. If he does, he soon moves away from his general audience and their general concerns. Every individual, after all, is more or less crazy; individual psychology is abnormal psychology. (Or, to put it another way: happy minds are all alike; every unhappy mind is unhappy in its own way.)

The Romantic period had encouraged everyone, readers and poets alike, to look deeply into their own minds. Appalled or merely bored by what they found there, many people turned back to public life, demanding poetry about people involved in social events. What they wanted, essentially, were short stories and novels in verse. Other people, including many poets, were fascinated by the haunted caverns of the mind, and they set out to chart its inversions and perversions, its twists and turns. This is, in essence, the story of nineteenth-century poetry: its division into the public poetry with which such writers as Robert Browning, Alfred, Lord Tennyson, and Walt Whitman tried to reach a wide, middle-class audience; and the private and often difficult poetry written by explorers of the individual psyche—especially Charles Baudelaire, Arthur Rimbaud, and Emily Dickinson.

Robert Browning (1812–1889) was the younger of the two great poets of Victorian England, and he seems to many modern readers almost the equal of Tennyson. He had an exuberantly happy and productive childhood, full of precocious achievements—discovering Byron's poetry when he was twelve, he immediately wrote a whole book of imitative poems—and he displayed from the start an intense

energy. In his first published book, *Pauline* (1833), his hero speaks for him in claiming a truly Faustian ambition:

> I am made up of an intensest life,
> ... [linked] to a principle of restlessness
> Which would be all, have, see, know, taste, feel, all—
> This is myself.

Not a single copy of *Pauline* was sold, and at least in retrospect that total failure seems to have had a decisive impact upon the author. Although Browning would go on writing long narratives in verse and attempting vainly to succeed as a dramatist, he would do his best work in dramatic monologues—verse speeches in which people of great but thwarted or misunderstood energy talk about themselves and their ideas, talk exuberantly, wildly, vividly, but talk . . . just talk. During his long creative life Browning gave birth to dozens of these striking individuals, but even in his dramatic poems *Sordello* and *The Ring and the Book* each character can make only the slightest of contacts with the outside world. Although their monologues are dramatic—someone else is usually there—these characters are really just talking to themselves. Browning titled two of his early adventures in abnormal psychology *Madhouse Cells*, and sometimes the title seems to apply to most of his work—where, behind mask after mask, his thwarted Faustian energy buzzes like a hornet in a bottle.

It buzzes most fiercely in the speeches of characters who are coarse and low-bred and therefore permitted to rail against the world, as he lets Caliban curse at his nasty creator-god Setebos—until a thunderstorm drives Caliban into a mindless frenzy of fear and repentance:

> What, what? A curtain o'er the world at once!
> Crickets stop hissing; not a bird—or, yes,
> There scuds His raven that has told Him all!
> It was fool's play this prattling! Ha! The wind
> Shoulders the pillared dust, death's house o' the move,
> And fast invading fires begin! White blaze—
> A tree's head snaps—and there, there, there, there, there,
> His thunder follows! Fool to gibe at Him!
> Lo! 'Lieth flat and loveth Setebos!
> 'Maketh his teeth meet through his upper lip,
> Will let those quails fly, will not eat this month
> One little mess of whelks, so he may 'scape!

But it was not this side of Browning's nature that won the heart of the forty-year-old invalid poetess Elizabeth Barrett when the thirty-four-year-old poet secretly married her and fled with her to Italy; it was not this side that made him a sought-after figure in English society when, after his wife's death, he returned from exile; and it was not this side that led to the forming in 1881 of the Browning Society, branches of which met around the world to worship their master's verse. Browning's reputation as a poet—now based upon his frustrated and abnormal characters—was then based upon his more optimistic people, such as that Rabbi Ben Ezra who cheerily cries:

The courtship and marriage of Robert Browning (left) and Elizabeth Barrett (below) is one of the most famous romances in literary history. During their fifteen years together, Elizabeth completed the masterpiece of her career, the series of love poems entitled Sonnets from the Portuguese. *For Robert Browning this period was less productive. It was not until his return to England from Italy following Elizabeth's death in 1861 that Browning began to reach his artistic maturity.*

> Grow old along with me!
> The best is yet to be,
> The last of life, for which the first was made!

The rabbi welcomes an old age full of care and doubt because those troubles demonstrate that we are not mere animals. ("Irks care the crop-full bird?/Frets doubt the maw-crammed beast?") Few of us now either need or welcome such a demonstration, but Browning was writing shortly after Darwin had suggested that we were descended from the apes, and Victorian society had little appetite for the idea. They wanted to believe that they were spiritual and that life was noble, heroic, clean, and under their control; and their poets often jollied them along. Browning was not the only one to strike a grand attitude for them, even in the face of death:

> I was ever a fighter, so—one fight more,
> The best and the last!

The pose was common; we remember William Ernest Henley's boast, for instance:

> It matters not how strait the gate,
> How charged with punishments the scroll,
> I am the master of my fate:
> I am the captain of my soul.

Yet even before Darwin's *Origin of Species*, the geologists and the Higher Criticism were raising havoc with old certainties and biblical

truths; the Reverend Thomas Robert Malthus had already preached the necessities of war, famine, pestilence, and death as checks on over-population; psychologists and philosophers were mapping out huge areas of determinism in our lives; and Karl Marx was hard at work in the British Museum. Victorian civilization was about to prove far less stable than the Roman Empire, try as its poets might to preserve the old certainties and the status quo.

None tried harder than Alfred, Lord Tennyson (1809–1892). He too wrote his poem about heroism in the face of death:

> Sunset and evening star,
>   And one clear call for me!
> And may there be no moaning of the bar,
>   When I put out to sea . . .

But most of his attitudes were less melodramatic than this, and his attempt to live up to his role as poet laureate made him the only man since Dryden to wear that title with much dignity. In later life he told a friend, "I soon found that if I meant to make any mark at all it must be by shortness, for all the men before me had been so diffuse, and all the big things had been done." By shortness, the author of *Idylls of the King, Enoch Arden,* and *In Memoriam* meant simply to refuse the challenge of the epic in favor of brief and highly polished poems. "To get the workmanship as nearly perfect as possible," he said, "is the best chance for going down the stream of time. A small vessel on fine lines is likely to float further than a great raft."

Appropriately for such a cautious conservative, his models were classical. Aspiring to be the Vergil of his age and country, he wrote the finest tribute to that poet since Dante:

> Roman Virgil, thou that singest
>   Ilion's lofty temples robed in fire,
> Ilion falling, Rome arising,
>   wars, and filial faith, and Dido's pyre;
>
> Landscape-lover, lord of language,
>   more than he that sang the "Works and Days,"
> All the chosen coin of fancy
>   flashing out from many a golden phrase . . .
>
> Thou that seest Universal
>   Nature moved by Universal Mind;
> Thou majestic in thy sadness
>   at the doubtful doom of human kind;
>
> Light among the vanish'd ages;
>   star that gildest yet this phantom shore;
> Golden branch amid the shadows,
>   kings and realms that pass to rise no more . . .
>
> I salute thee, Mantovano,
>   I that loved thee since my day began,
> Wielder of the stateliest measure
>   ever moulded by the lips of man.

Following the publication of The Ring and the Book *in 1869, Browning's reputation as a leading poet of his age was secured, and he found himself increasingly involved in social rather than literary activities. The Browning Society was founded in London in 1881, and soon branches were meeting there and throughout the world to venerate the poet and his works. In the cartoon opposite, Max Beerbohm portrays one of these gatherings with the object of their worship, Browning himself, joining his admirers for tea.*

Few poets have represented the tenor of the times in which they lived quite so well as Alfred, Lord Tennyson (photograph at left by Julia Margaret Cameron). On political and social questions, Tennyson shared the Victorian era's apprehension about the changes that could be seen developing on all sides. One of his most ambitious projects was a reinterpretation of the Arthurian legends, Idylls of the King *(Doré engraving of Camelot opposite), which was a popular but not a critical success.*

The comparison is more suggestive than Tennyson might wish to realize, for the qualities that he praises in Vergil—his craftsmanship, his affection for nature, his concern with the past, and especially his majestic sadness—all these are Tennyson's primary qualities too. For all his patriotism, Vergil had surely been reluctant to take on the writing of the *Aeneid*, and Tennyson's bardship was equally reluctant. "The night before I was asked to take the Laureateship, which was offered to me through Prince Albert's liking for my *In Memoriam*, I dreamed that he came to me and kissed me on the cheek," Tennyson told a friend. "I said, in my dream, 'Very kind, but very German.' In the morning the letter about the Laureateship was brought to me and laid upon my bed. I thought about it through the day but could not make up my mind whether to take it or refuse it, and at the last I wrote two letters, one accepting and one declining, and threw them on the table, and settled to decide which I would send after my dinner and bottle of port."

In 1833 his greatly loved friend Arthur Henry Hallam had died unexpectedly, plunging Tennyson into a decade and more of grief that interfered greatly with his life (engaged in 1838, he postponed marriage until 1850) but also produced a torrent of fine melancholy poetry, including *Ulysses, Tithonus, Morte d'Arthur* and other parts of *Idylls of the King,* and especially the more than 130 poems collected as *In Memoriam.* That poem swelled in the writing from a series of personal laments with no greater message than that " 'Tis better to have loved and lost, / Than never to have loved at all," into a public work with a cosmic conclusion focused on

> That God, which ever lives and loves,
> One God, one law, one element,
> And one far-off divine event
> To which the whole creation moves.

Tennyson told a friend that *In Memoriam* "begins with a funeral and ends with a marriage—begins with death and ends in a promise of a new life—a sort of Divine Comedy, cheerful at the close." This grandiose evaluation of what he had earlier called "short swallow-flights of song" reminds us that the poem epitomizes his whole career, his evolution from the young poet of personal melancholy to the poet laureate and peer of the realm who labored so diligently in later life to lead his readers to truth and God, urging them—despite Darwin's discoveries—to

> . . . Arise and fly
> The reeling Faun, the sensual feast;
> Move upward, working out the beast,
> And let the ape and tiger die.

Meanwhile, his contemporary Browning was following the same path from poet to sage, and in France Tennyson's equal Victor Hugo

The tragic drowning of his daughter Léopoldine in the sea at Villequier in 1843 cast Victor Hugo (photograph at lower left) into the depths of sorrow and despondency. He nursed his grief in private and in writing, dedicating a book of verse entitled Les Contemplations *to her memory. The moody and sensitive poems of* Les Feuilles D'Automne *(below) were a product of Hugo's hurt and disappointment over the breakup of his marriage. The poet's enormous emotional and intellectual range enabled him to produce poems of overwhelming intimacy and delicacy as well as those of tremendous political and social impact. The latter include* La Légende des Siècles *(frontispiece designed by Hugo himself, opposite).*

LES
FEUILLES
D'AUTOMNE.

Si vous voulez, à l'heure où la lune décline,
Nous monterons tous deux la nuit sur la colline
Où gisent nos aïeux.

Page 56.

LA
LEGENDE
DES
SIECLES

Au Poëte exquis,
au cœur grand et charmant,
à Paul Meurice!
Victor Hugo

H.H. 1ª janvier
1860

(1802–1885) was close behind. Starting with little interest in anything but moods, passions, and beautiful verse, Hugo soon involved himself in politics, made himself France's unofficial poet laureate, took her destiny on his shoulders, and by the end of his life was writing large and obscure visionary poems with such titles as *The Trumpet of Judgment*, *The End of Satan*, and *God*. The lives of all three men were to demonstrate the dangers of popularity for a poet. Tennyson's funeral, for example, was a public occasion comparable to the greatest stage triumphs of Charles Dickens. Browning, as has been noted, had his Browning Society; and Hugo ended his days as a senator of the Third Republic. But all this public success was based on a dangerous misconception of poetry.

Since the time of the Puritans, defenders of poetry have tried to clear its name by insisting that it is morally safe, and even that it teaches us how to live well and be good citizens. Perhaps they are right, unlikely as the idea seems. But when poets believe such talk they are all too likely to abandon poetry in favor of didactic verse like Tennyson's passages above—verse demanding not merely that we participate in the experience of the poem but that we accept and adopt the poet's notions about life. This will never do. The ability to write verse well has no necessary connection with wisdom or even with knowledge; Tennyson and Hugo, in particular, possessed strikingly commonplace minds. That may help to account for their widespread popularity, but at the same time it obliges us to discount their didacticism. Like Alexander Pope, they merely speak for their age, expressing—often with great eloquence and charm—what oft was thought but ne'er so well expressed.

While these poets composed emotions and ideas for an audience ripe to sympathize, other poets were seeking within themselves for new ideas and even new emotions. Their researches were imitated in England, with shrill schoolboy naughtiness, by Algernon Charles Swinburne (1837–1909). Unfortunately his rhapsodies about kisses that sting and our lady of pain, though beautifully versified, have lost their thrill in our coarser and more nearly honest age, as have his railings at Christianity ("Thou hast conquered, O pale Galilean; the world has grown gray from thy breath"). What remains is primarily his ability, the equal of Tennyson's, to express our favorite sentimentalities in limpid verse:

> From too much love of living,
>> From hope and fear set free,
> We thank with brief thanksgiving
>> Whatever gods may be
> That no life lives for ever;
> That dead men rise up never;
> That even the weariest river
>> Winds somewhere safe to sea.

Sentimentality is a relatively normal aberration. They disordered these things differently in France, and more seriously—especially in the life and verses of Charles Baudelaire (1821–1867). Although

French poetry had caught the enthusiasm generated by the Romantic movement in the arts, it had caught little of its critical and philosophic intensity, and Baudelaire inherited an oddly simple sort of French Romantic verse. How limited it was is most quickly suggested by his enthusiastic response to the verse, fiction, and criticism of Edgar Allen Poe, whom Baudelaire took to be a genius in these fields. (In fact, Poe is a derivative and reductive imitator in all fields but that of the detective story.) What matters in Poe's graveyard morbidity and his Byronesque concern with incest and abnormal psychology is primarily that they licensed Baudelaire's own plunge into the dark and dank recesses of his mind in search of new excitements, new knowledge, and new sensations, and that they certified these subjects as proper material for poetry.

Francis Bacon—Baron Verulam, Viscount St. Albans, Lord Chancellor of England, and convicted bribe-taker, whom Pope called "the wisest, brightest, meanest of mankind"—wrote that "there is no excellent beauty that hath not some strangeness in the proportion." Where classical artists had sought for beauty in the perfect norm, and Romanticists had seen it in the intensely lovable, Baudelaire sought that strangeness-in-beauty that Bacon had perceived, and he found it not in the Walt Disney ghost-story images of Poe but in himself and in the contemporary world. As he wrote about *The Flowers of Evil*: "Certain illustrious poets have long since divided among themselves the more flowery provinces of the realm of poetry. I have found it amusing, and the more pleasant because the task was more difficult, to extract *beauty* from *Evil*."

Torn since childhood between "the horror of living and the ecstasy of living," and convinced that "the Beautiful is always bizarre," Baudelaire wrote poems of great formal elegance, rhythmic and sonorous but concerned with grotesque and distasteful subjects. Novelist Marcel Proust fittingly described *The Flowers of Evil* as "that sublime but sardonic book in which piety sneers, in which debauchery makes the sign of the cross, in which Satan is entrusted with the task of teaching the most profound theology." A sniff at one blossom from that bouquet will probably suffice most readers; this is from *The Carrion*:

> My dear, remember what you saw that day,
>   that summer morn so fair and sweet:
> next to the path a ghastly carcass lay
>   bedded in gravel at your feet,
>
> with her legs cocked up like some lubricious slut,
>   cooking and sweating poisons there,
> nonchalantly, cynically, her gut
>   exhaled its stenches to the air . . .
>
> —Yet you'll be like this stinking carrion,
>   this vile infection here,
> beautiful star of my eyes, my nature's sun,
>   my passion, angel, dear!

The whimsical caricature above depicts Algernon Charles Swinburne, the innovative English poet who rebelled against the morals and manners of the Victorian society in which he lived.

Les Fleurs du Mal, *the single book of verse produced by Charles Baudelaire, is filled with vivid, macabre images that have stirred the imaginations of numerous artists. The illustration for the poem* Le Fantôme *(far left) appeared in an 1899 edition of the work. A likeness of Baudelaire is seen in the watercolor at near left, but a more sensitive portrait (above) was painted by Gustave Courbet. One of the finest French lyrical poets, Paul Verlaine was left a broken and dissolute man after his two-year liaison with Arthur Rimbaud. The pair is seen at the extreme left in the Fantin-Latour work (left, above)* Le Coin de Table.

> . . . Ah then, O my beauty, to each worm
>   who kisses you and eats you, say
>   that I've kept still the pure, essential form
>   of all my loves that rot away!

To be sure, this is essentially what Shakespeare meant when he boasted:

> Yet do thy worst, old Time: despite thy wrong,
> My love shall in my verse ever live young.

But Baudelaire found a way to add strangeness to that beauty and to make beauty a difficult conception of the mind rather than a simple quality in things. Yet despite the drugs and alcohol and syphilis that were to destroy him, Baudelaire was not corrupted by the evil he found in himself and outside himself. An expert in sin, he retained his vision of goodness and innocence and could evoke them as he did in the sweet melancholy with which he begins *Le Voyage*:

> The child in love with maps and prints can see
>   a world that matches his vast appetite.
> How small it is when seen in memory
>   that was so grand beneath the study's light!

Ulalume — A Ballad.
By Edgar A. Poe.

The skies they were ashen and sober;
  The leaves they were crispéd and sere —
  The leaves they were withering and sere:
It was night, in the lonesome October
  Of my most immemorial year:
It was hard by the dim lake of Auber,
  In the misty mid region of Weir: —
It was down by the dank tarn of Auber,
  In the ghoul-haunted woodland of Weir.

Here once, through an alley Titanic,
  Of cypress, I roamed with my Soul —
  Of cypress, with Psyche, my Soul.
These were days when my heart was volcanic
  As the scoriac rivers that roll —
  As the lavas that restlessly roll
Their sulphurous currents down Yaanek,
  In the ultimate climes of the Pole —
That groan as they roll down Mount Yaanek,
  In the realms of the Boreal Pole.

Our talk had been serious and sober,
  But our thoughts they were palsied and sere —
  Our memories were treacherous and sere;

Today Edgar Allan Poe (*shown above, left, in a Mathew Brady daguerreotype*) is recognized as one of the most creative literary minds the United States has produced. But during his lifetime such acclaim and encouragement as he did receive came mainly from abroad, and especially from the French Symbolist poets Baudelaire, Verlaine, Rimbaud, and Mallarmé. Although Poe published three collections of poetry by the time he was twenty-two, he then abandoned verse until shortly before his death, when he wrote his final masterpieces, The Raven (*Manet engraving above*), Ulalume (*manuscript at left*), and Annabel Lee.

Many of Baudelaire's followers modeled their lives as well as their attitude toward poetry on his, experimenting with—and sometimes destroying themselves with—alcohol, drugs, and unorthodox sexuality. Among these the most talented were that strange pair Paul Verlaine (1844–1896) and Arthur Rimbaud (1854–1891). Their poetry is as dissimilar as possible: Verlaine is essentially lyrical and moody, while Rimbaud is a wild extremist, ranging in his verse from sentimental childhood fantasies to almost incoherent hallucinations. In their serio-comic, intermittent love affair, however, it was Verlaine who behaved the more extremely: at one point Rimbaud unaffectionately had the older poet imprisoned in a Flemish jail for having shot him in the arm. Verlaine's life ended in aimless and alcoholic poverty; Rimbaud died in his hometown, of gangrene from an amputated leg, almost twenty years after he had abandoned his brilliant poetry to wander the world as, among other things, a deserter from the Dutch army in Batavia, an interpreter and manager of a European circus, and an African trader and gun-runner.

Meanwhile, across the ocean and safely sheltered from all this rebellion and debauchery, a lonely woman in the seemingly proper college town of Amherst, Massachusetts, was demonstrating that if unbridled overindulgence can produce insights into the stranger rooms of the mind, a sensitive and alert abstinence can also open up many haunted passages. Emily Dickinson (1830–1886) was one of several children of a prominent, forceful, and pious Amherst citizen. She spent almost a year at nearby Mount Holyoke Academy, where she was cheerful and popular but where she began to encounter the first serious signs of her difference from other people. A religious "awakening" was sweeping the region at the time, and only Emily held out. "The path of duty looks very ugly indeed—" she wrote in her journal, "and the place where *I* want to go more amiable —a great deal—it is so much easier to do wrong than right—so much pleasanter to be evil than good, I don't wonder that good angels weep —and bad ones sing songs."

Her family and friends did not understand such reasoning, and so Dickinson began her lifelong process of shutting out the world by leaving Mount Holyoke for home. Blake would have understood her comments, as would Mark Twain; Baudelaire would have misunderstood and approved—but she was essentially different from these people. Like Blake, she had a great interest in Nobodaddy and little affection for him (she said that her pious family "address an Eclipse, every morning—whom they call their Father"); but she herself, unlike Blake, firmly believed in repression, renunciation, and suffering.

Goethe's Faust had chosen to league himself with the devil out of frustration at society's repressiveness:

You must renounce! Renounce you must!
This is the everlasting song
That always tinkles in our ears,
Passionately and lifelong
Singing to us through the years.

Overleaf: *The literary salons held in Victor Hugo's home were well-attended and important social events in the mid-nineteenth century.*

Dickinson went in the other direction, took matters out of society's hands, and so crushed her own life that in her later years she could say: "I do not cross my father's ground to any house or town." Such an excess brought its own intensities of feeling. "Renunciation—is a piercing Virtue," she wrote, preferring great pain to insipid pleasures but also painfully afraid of being hurt from outside. "The Missing All—prevented Me/From missing minor Things," she observed: if she renounced a loved one completely, he could not fail her across the breakfast table. And so she fell in love with inaccessible people, worshiped from afar, and poured her feelings into handstitched collections of poems kept mostly to herself. (Only seven of the works were published in her lifetime—out of almost 1,800 that had been written.) Like Goethe's Faust, she knew that anticipation is keener than achievement, though she much preferred to increase the keenness by pretending to believe the opposite:

> It might be easier
> To fail—with Land in Sight—
> Than gain—My Blue Peninsula—
> To perish—of Delight . . .

In the seclusion of her room, from which she rarely ventured except on flights of pure imagination, Emily Dickinson created an extraordinary body of aphoristic verse. Only a handful of those untitled poems were published during her lifetime; all of them, like Two Were Immortal Twice, at left, are identified only by their opening lines. At upper right, a rare photograph of Amherst's most famous literary recluse.

120

She knew, though, that it is only distance that lends the enchantment of blue to what might be all too brown and rocky a reality, some dry spit of land. Recognizing that, she speculated once that God might be acting kindly in moving one of her fancied lovers from Philadelphia to San Francisco

> To spare these Striding Spirits
> Some Morning of Chagrin—
> The waking in a Gnat's embrace—
> Our Giants—further on . . .

Dickinson never woke in anyone's embrace, and thereby spared herself gnats and left herself free to dream and suffer intensely. The poems she made out of her imagined losses often express great pain, but they deal with dreams rather than experience, and this unreality allows her some sadly melodramatic exaggeration. Shelley fancied himself "a herd-abandoned deer struck by the hunter's dart," and Dickinson styled herself "Empress of Calvary" and wore a white dress winter and summer to indicate the number of tribulations she had overcome. She had a finely developed sense of humor, though, about other things:

> She sights a Bird—she chuckles—
> She flattens—then she crawls—
> She runs without the look of feet—
> Her eyes increase to Balls—
>
> Her Jaws stir—twitching—hungry—
> Her Teeth can hardly stand—
> She leaps, but Robin leaped the first—
> Ah, Pussy, of the Sand—
>
> The Hopes so juicy ripening—
> You almost bathed your Tongue—
> When Bliss disclosed a hundred Toes—
> And fled with every one . . .

Emily didn't like cats much, so she could be funny about their failures. To find her own failures equally amusing was generally beyond her, as it was beyond most nineteenth-century poets. When the French Symbolist poet Jules Laforgue (1860–1887), in his *Complaint of Lord Pierrot*, clowned about his own inadequacies, he sounded almost the first notes of a self-deprecating comic irony that the twentieth century would learn to prize highly:

> Ah! some eve, if one should bring of her own will herself,
> Desiring only to drink at my lips, or kill herself!
>
> I would be the most noble conquest, don't you know,
> That woman exalted by Dream ever brought low!
>
> Till then my ambition rises
> Just to life's old compromises . . .

H.W.L. "in the clouds"
at Göttingen!

In the middle decades of the nineteenth century, American poetry was to enjoy an unprecedented efflorescence. Led by Henry Wadsworth Longfellow (far left, below), native American writers were to produce the new nation's first popular verse—and in so doing establish a true native mythology. Longfellow, who sketched the comical self-portrait at far left, above, in 1829, drew upon New World legends for the long narrative poems—such as Evangeline, Hiawatha, and The Courtship of Miles Standish—that brought poetry its appreciative new audience. Critics argued the merits of Longfellow's self-consciously literary verse, but the public did not: he was the best-loved and most widely translated poet of his day. Although he wrote poetry steadily throughout his life, Longfellow's contemporary John Greenleaf Whittier (near left) was by no means exclusively a poet. As a newspaper editor, abolitionist pamphleteer, and member of the Massachusetts legislature he produced a steady stream of nonfiction as well. Indeed, it was not until after the Civil War ended that Whittier found time to compose his winter idyll, Snow-bound. (At lower left is the snow-blanketed frame house in which "the voice of rural New England" wrote his best-known work.) The most strikingly original poet of this period did not publish a single line of verse until he was thirty-six. In fact, there was little about the early career of Walt Whitman (below, left), a sometime teacher and editor of the Brooklyn Eagle, to prepare the literary world for his remarkable volume Leaves of Grass, issued in 1855. Many readers found Whitman's poems vulgar, but the work as a whole won unqualified endorsement from aging transcendentalist poet Ralph Waldo Emerson. "The bard of democracy," is the subject of the Beerbohm caricature at lower right entitled Walt Whitman Inciting the Bird of Freedom to Soar.

7

The Modern Renaissance

During the half century that he practiced medicine in Rutherford, New Jersey, William Carlos Williams found time to write numerous novels, short stories, plays, essays, and poems. It is for the latter that he is chiefly remembered, of course, and it was for his precise perceptions of everyday urban life that he was awarded the Pulitzer Prize for poetry in 1963. The painting opposite, Charles Demuth's I Saw the Figure 5 in Gold, *was inspired by a Williams poem entitled* The Great Figure.

DESPITE THEIR DESIRE to make readers into good citizens, most nineteenth-century poets had emphasized not the citizen but the self—and Browning, Baudelaire, and Dickinson were not alone in stressing the loneliness and isolation of the self from society, from good citizenship, and even, at our deepest moments, from morality and rational thought. "The mind resorts to reason for lack of training," as the American historian Henry Adams put it, and the artists of the last century trained their reader to find much more than reason in his mind. These artists also emphasized their own isolation and diversity: the public poets and bards of earlier times were now supplanted by lonely individuals; and John Butler Yeats summed up that change when he wrote that "a work of art is the social act of a solitary man." This sense of irrational solitude, along with emphasis on the permissible diversity of poetic styles and the insignificance of public life, constitutes the chief inheritance of twentieth-century poets.

Ours is a century of supernations, the third world, international wars and economic struggles, enforced conformity in thought and behavior, and a destiny manifest even in the daily newspaper. In such a century this poetic inheritance may seem thoroughly useless, like shares in a buggy-whip factory. In fact, however, it is an extremely valuable possession, almost a magic charm against many of the central ills of our culture.

A century and a half ago William Hazlitt observed that if the human race really wished to be good it would long ago have become so. But except in medicine and tools, we do not improve. Patriotism has been revealed as the last refuge of scoundrels, yet it is still touted as a virtue today. Nationalism has been a persistent cause of economic, political, and military strife, especially since the advent of Joan of Arc, yet new nations emerge every year. War has been exposed as no heroic, Homeric activity but as a savage means of contending for economic and political advantage, yet it is still celebrated today. Obedience to external rules has been proved a weak and psychologically dangerous substitute for internal and individual morality, yet law and order—often enforced by hypocrites—pervade our lives. And although completely developed individual psyches are the basis of any approvable life, our educational systems, such as they are, still emphasize conformity, mass obedience, and reverence for authority.

Against these influences and others, all of them dangerous to the enjoyment of our tightrope walk through time and space, poetry in our century provides a valuable if not a guaranteed defense. Twentieth-century poets have sought to preserve and strengthen our precious individuality, speaking to our personal faculties and feelings. Yet precisely because those faculties and feelings are so central, they have made us aware, simultaneously, of the individual self and of a brotherhood of man far more credible and valuable than those arbitrary groupings imposed by race, sex, color, nation, or creed.

In a time when much of our cultural heritage has been cheapened or obscured, and when totally new and unexplored sources of truth have been opened widely to the Western world—most notably the arts and religions of the East—poets have labored to expand our awareness of both old and new values. In his monumental *Four Quartets*, for instance, T. S. Eliot brings together Christian myths, seventeenth-century English history, *Alice in Wonderland*, the *Bhagavad-Gita*, and a wide range of poets and mystics. He does so not to flaunt his individual knowledge but to emphasize the unity that orders our apparently fragmentary accumulation of images and truths—a task also undertaken, on a far grander scale, by Ezra Pound in his *Cantos*.

For Eliot, Christianity was a primary source of ideas and images. For Pound, history was primary; for Yeats, the hermetic truths of Eastern thought and of the Kabalah; for Wallace Stevens, the discoveries of Romantic poets and French painters. There are, of course, many other sources and many other poets to exploit them; not since Elizabethan times has poetry—especially poetry in English—found voices so marvelous and so diversified as in this century.

Although this is a time when systems—nationalism, capitalism, fascism, and communism, among others—overwhelm public life, it is also an age in which traditional social, political, economic, and religious systems have grown increasingly less persuasive. Mobs of people still profess belief in them, it is true, but less out of conviction than out of a desperate desire to believe in something, anything.

This desire to believe cannot be argued with; as John Butler Yeats observed, "when a belief rests upon nothing you cannot knock away its foundations." Many of our poets therefore show little interest in such inflated subjects, preferring to trust in immediate experience, however fragmentary, and to write personally and lyrically about isolated moments of existence. Thomas Hardy, D. H. Lawrence, Robert Frost, E. E. Cummings, Theodore Roethke, John Crowe Ransom . . . the list could be extended indefinitely of those modern poets who have made us see, feel, and comprehend those moments of life that, paradoxically, we have all experienced in different ways together. The transitory fragility of youth, for example, is an age-old theme, but Ransom renews it for us in his *Blue Girls*:

> Twirling your blue skirts, traveling the sward
> Under the towers of your seminary,
> Go listen to your teachers old and contrary
> Without believing a word.

Tie the white fillets then about your hair
And think no more of what will come to pass
Than bluebirds that go walking on the grass
And chattering on the air.

Practise your beauty, blue girls, before it fail;
And I will cry with my loud lips and publish
Beauty which all our power shall never establish,
It is so frail.

For I could tell you a story which is true;
I know a lady with a terrible tongue,
Blear eyes fallen from blue,
All her perfections tarnished—yet it is not long
Since she was lovelier than any of you.

The theme is perennial, but we are Elizabethan in our concern with mutability as a falling off rather than as growth into maturity. Even that moralist T. S. Eliot felt the loss in his *New Hampshire* landscape:

Children's voices in the orchard
Between the blossom- and the fruit-time:
Golden head, crimson head,
Between the green tip and the root.
Black wing, brown wing, hover over;
Twenty years and the spring is over;
Today grieves, tomorrow grieves,
Cover me over, light-in-leaves;
Golden head, black wing,
Cling, swing,
Spring, sing,
Swing up into the apple-tree.

Both these poems are occasional—that is, they focus on specific occasions experienced or imagined by the poet. The most important poetry seeks a larger scope than this, however. Traditionally, the poet who wished to speak at length on great issues chose occasions of great political and military significance and characters of heroic dimensions. In our time we are skeptical of such people and occasions, and our poets have often turned to other means of expanding their perceptions and embodying their truths. Most characteristically, they have turned to using symbols.

Despite their high-class name, symbols are actually simple things; we all use them every day and could hardly get along without them. For the poet they constitute a way to avoid the limitations of occasional verse and of individuality and subjectivity, while still staying in the world of the mind. A bird, a tree, a river are merely natural objects in themselves, but when we add to them the meanings imposed upon them by man down through the ages, they become magically natural and human at once. Swinburne, for instance, assured us that life will not drag on forever by reminding us that "even the weariest

Thomas Hardy (above) had firmly established his reputation as one of England's leading novelists when, in 1898, he abandoned prose fiction altogether to concentrate on poetry. In the last thirty years of his life Hardy produced eight volumes of extremely idiosyncratic and highly colloquial verse. D.H. Lawrence (left), on the other hand, began his career as a poet and created a large private bestiary—including Fish, Snake, *and* Mountain Lion—*before turning to the long and often turgid novels that brought him notoriety. American poet John Crowe Ransom (left, above) is likewise hard to classify. A prominent poet of the Southern agrarian school, he was also an influential essayist and editor.*

river winds somewhere safe to sea." This river image expresses not just Swinburne's personal notion but a generally shared belief, and as a result we do not respond by wondering why he is talking about rivers. We understand him at once: life *is* like a river. And when Catholics envision the Holy Spirit as a dove, or angels as winged, we are likewise unsurprised; air seems to be the natural domain of the spirit, and birds control the air. Christian orthodoxy asserts that a dove and Mary produced Jesus, and Greek mythology holds that Leda and Zeus engendered Helen of Troy (with Zeus taking the form of a swan in order to do so). Both stories seem immediately intelligible; in both, the birdlike spirit must combine with the fertile flesh of woman to embody its truths.

Among modern poets it was William Butler Yeats (1865–1939) who most fully explored the symbolic meanings in our world, and birds are among his central concerns. He saw Greek and Greco-Roman civilizations as derived from the Trojan War, but he treated the subject neither like Homer nor like a modern historian. Instead, he focused on the images at the heart of that war, and especially on the beautiful woman

The convivial group at left, gathered at a New York literary bistro known as Petipa's, includes the Irish painter John Butler Yeats (second from left). Yeats' son William, seen at right in a portrait executed by his father in 1900, briefly tried his hand at painting before turning to poetry. His subsequent output earned the younger Yeats a place among the giants of twentieth-century poetry—and the dubious honor of being lampooned by Max Beerbohm. In the caricature below, the lanky poet is shown introducing fellow Dubliner George Moore (with Yeats a co-founder of the famed Abbey Theatre) to the Queen of the Fairies.

over whom it was fought. What truths and values did Helen embody? His poem *Leda and the Swan* raises the question:

> A sudden blow: the great wings beating still
> Above the staggering girl, her thighs caressed
> By the dark webs, her nape caught in his bill,
> He holds her helpless breast upon his breast.
>
> How can those terrified vague fingers push
> The feathered glory from her loosening thighs?
> And how can body, laid in that white rush,
> But feel the strange heart beating where it lies?
>
> A shudder in the loins engenders there
> The broken wall, the burning roof and tower
> And Agamemnon dead.
>   Being so caught up,
> So mastered by the brute blood of the air,
> Did she put on his knowledge with his power
> Before the indifferent beak could let her drop?

One of the principal concerns of Yeats' life—nationalism—was exemplified in the remarkable life of Maud Gonne (right), a legendary figure in Ireland's struggle for independence. Gonne, a patriot and philanthropist whose husband was executed after the bloody Easter Rebellion of 1916 (far right), was an enduring source of inspiration for Yeats, who made her the heroine of numerous plays and poems. The drawing at left, which appeared in a 1920 edition of Vanity Fair, records a poetry reading attended by Yeats, Robert Nichols, Siegfried Sassoon, and other literary figures of the day.

A bird can also give form to the spirit of our present age, and since that spirit is one of uncontrollable destructive force, Yeats can imagine it as a bird of prey out of control:

> Turning and turning in the widening gyre
> The falcon cannot hear the falconer;
> Things fall apart; the centre cannot hold;
> Mere anarchy is loosed upon the world . . .

Yet our own personal spirits need not be dangerous. Praying for his infant daughter, Yeats embodies his hopes for her spirit and body in the image of a happy songbird in a laurel tree:

> May she become a flourishing hidden tree
> That all her thoughts may like the linnet be . . .

In his own life, Yeats associated his beloved and beautiful Maud Gonne with that desirable daughter of Leda and the swan, Helen of Troy; and standing among schoolchildren Yeats uses this association to think of Maud as a swan's child among ducklings:

I look upon one child or t'other there
And wonder if she stood so at that age—
For even daughters of the swan can share
Something of every paddler's heritage . . .

And in old age, having become an old scarecrow whose withered body is frightening his spirit away, Yeats imagines a timeless image for himself, the poet as an imperishable golden bird:

Once out of nature I shall never take
My bodily form from any natural thing,
But such a form as Grecian goldsmiths make
Of hammered gold and gold enamelling
To keep a drowsy Emperor awake;
Or set upon a golden bough to sing
To lords and ladies of Byzantium
Of what is past, or passing, or to come.

The man who wrote such fine verse and who handled symbols like a master magician played many parts during his long lifetime. Seeking for certainties beyond material facts, he spent five years as a member of Madame Blavatsky's Theosophical Society. Asked by her to leave because of his skepticism and his interest in experimental magic, he joined the Hermetic Students of the Rosicrucian Golden Dawn, studying the Kabala and working with magic emblems. Meanwhile, he was also becoming a central figure in the Irish Literary Society, which, after the downfall and death of Charles Stewart Parnell, gave political nationalism a nonpartisan outlet while exploring and encouraging Irish writers past and present. It was Yeats who kept the society from becoming merely a source of Irish propaganda. He could not stop the bad writers—no one has ever learned how to do that—but he did give such encouragement to the good ones that he began an Irish renaissance, in fiction and drama as well as in poetry, that was to prove a chief literary event of our century.

Yeats was also a founder of what would become the Abbey Theatre, and he was a reluctant but effective member of the politically active Irish Republican Brotherhood. He joined this organization mainly to impress Maud Gonne, whom he had met in 1889. She was a year younger, six feet tall, strikingly beautiful, and devoted to revolutionary politics. (She was said to carry a hand grenade in her purse.) For half his working life Yeats poured out a flood of fine love poetry as he pursued her—unsuccessfully. His love moved the shy young poet into the public life of Ireland, and thereby inspired many fine political and public poems in addition to the cultural work for which, in 1922, he was named a senator of the Irish Free State. One year later he won the Nobel Prize for Literature, confirming his public role and testifying to his international importance. But the poet in him and the vigorous man in him never faded away. At the age of sixty-six he wrote a friend, "I shall be a sinful man to the end, and think upon my deathbed of all the nights I wasted in my youth." And to the end he continued to write better and better poetry, shaping and making intelligible our chaotic world more successfully than any poet had previously done in English.

In a letter written only a week before he died, Yeats phrased his finest justification of art. "Man can embody truth," he wrote, "but he cannot know it." Didactic philosophy and conscious knowledge deal in limited abstractions; only art can evoke the kaleidoscopic truths of life itself. Almost thirty years earlier he had written a finely ironic little poem about *The Coming of Wisdom with Time*:

> Though leaves are many, the root is one;
> Through all the lying days of my youth
> I swayed my leaves and flowers in the sun;
> Now I may wither into the truth.

With time Yeats came to learn, and to teach us, that the leaves and flowers are as true as the root, and that the lies of our youth are as valid, if not as enduring, as the rooted truths of our old age. They all embody us, though no one of them can sum us up.

World War I, which devastated vast stretches of France and introduced full-scale trench warfare in the Lowlands (British painting, far right), also decimated Europe's literary landscape. Before Germany sued for peace in 1918, the war to end wars had claimed two of England's most promising young poets, Rupert Brooke (right, above) and Wilfred Owen (right), who was killed one week before the Armistice was signed. One of the survivors of this bloodletting was Robert Graves (above), whose prodigious output includes long historical novels as well as highly polished verse.

Of course Yeats did more with his symbols than exploit their individual implications; he built them into coherent forms and elaborate interpretations of life, especially in his prose work *A Vision*. The result has been widely misunderstood. His reduction of the material world to the elements of earth, air, fire, and water; his enclosure of meaning within such emblems as flower, bird, candle, and fish; and his ritualization of the flow of life into the phases of the moon or the interaction of gyres—all of this aroused the scorn of many elderly and conventional people, and it still does. But it intrigues the young, and rightly so, because these patterns of existence clarify and interweave experiences and perceptions that in youth are necessarily fragmentary and partial. Yeats was not a dull or an abstract man, but he knew that some kinds of knowledge can only be expressed generally—and even in *A Vision* he used images copiously to keep those generalities in touch with our sensual and imaginative experience of life.

The wisdom of poetry is difficult to define. Too often it is confused with the facts or ideas in a poem, and too often it is taken as demanding belief. Yeats kept his head clear. Introducing *A Vision*, he wrote: "Some will ask whether I believe in the actual existence of my circuits of sun and moon." His surprising answer hinges on the distinction between belief and the structure of thought: "To such a question I can but answer that if sometimes, overwhelmed by miracle as all men must be when in the midst of it, I have taken such periods literally, my reason has soon recovered; and now that the system stands out clearly in my imagination I regard them as stylistic arrangements of experience comparable to the cubes in the drawing of Wyndham Lewis and to the ovoids in the sculpture of Brancusi. They have helped me to hold in a single thought reality and justice." "Reality and justice"—what is and what ought to be. "Wisdom is a butterfly and not a gloomy bird of prey," Yeats wrote, and reality and justice are the extremes between which it flutters.

The poet who most resembles Yeats in his pursuit of this butterfly is Wallace Stevens (1879-1955), a lawyer and vice-president of a Hartford, Connecticut, insurance firm. His exuberant use of language is unmatched among American poets, as is his firm sense of the reality of thought. "The greatest poverty is not to live in a physical world," he wrote, but this physical world is merely the necessary condition of thought, not an end in itself:

> The poet striding among the cigar stores,
> Ryan's lunch, hatters, insurance and medicines,
> Denies that abstraction is a vice except
> To the fatuous. These are his infernal walls,
> A space of stone, of inexplicable base
> And peaks outsoaring possible adjectives.
> One man, the idea of man, that is the space,
> The true abstract in which he promenades.
> The era of the idea of man, the cloak
> And speech of Virgil dropped, that's where he walks . . .

The poem's description is quite literal. Stevens walked to work, composing as he went, and on arrival at the office would dictate the results to his secretary. She must often have been startled—one poem begins with an irritated and envious bantam trying to cut a strutting rooster down to size:

> Chieftain Iffucan of Azcan in caftan
> Of tan with henna hackles, halt!
>
> Damned universal cock, as if the sun
> Was blackamoor to bear your blazing tail . . .

The cock is any person whose imagination is vividly alive, especially the poet. For such people the external world shines far less brightly than their minds; the world serves them, not they the world—and ordinary people like the bantam find this irritating. But Stevens always celebrates the imagination; it is inexhaustible, dangerous, and ineffably rewarding. And it keeps us alert for those unexpected delights of life that cannot be planned or programmed:

> One's grand flights, one's Sunday baths,
> One's tootings at the weddings of the soul
> Occur as they occur.

Most importantly, Stevens reminds us that the creative mind is its own place, the external world merely its setting or its distraction:

> . . . this time, this day,
> It is a state, this spring among the politicians
> Playing cards. In a village of the indigenes,
> One would have still to discover. Among the dogs and dung,
> One would continue to contend with one's ideas.

Although he is always associated with New England, Robert Frost (above, right) was actually born in San Francisco, and his poem Once by the Pacific, *seen in draft form above, recounts an incident from his West Coast childhood. Frost's contemporary Wallace Stevens (left) is as firmly associated with Hartford, Connecticut, where he served for decades as an insurance company executive —a curious sort of occupation for a poet known for his vivid imagery and bold metaphors.*

Some poets have taken the external world more seriously, among them Robert Frost (1874–1963). Born in San Francisco, Frost was moved to New England at the age of eleven and promptly disguised himself as a native; for the rest of his life he wrote and spoke in the accents and often the dialects of New England country people. Partly for this reason and partly because his poems are filled with mountains, brooks, fields, trees, flowers, and birds, Frost is often mistaken for a New England nature poet. He is not, however; although he is often sentimental he seldom goes so far as to claim that nature has any close connections to mankind. When he talks to the tree at his window, he is as concerned with separation as with connection:

> That day she put our heads together,
> Fate had her imagination about her,
> Your head so much concerned with outer,
> Mine with inner, weather.

When Frost speaks more seriously of nature it is to warn us against the fallacy of believing that nature exists in human terms or that it even cares for human life. In verses with a characteristically punning title, Frost speaks of *The Need of Being Versed in Country Things.* These verses sketch a burned-out farmhouse and a deserted barn, evoke the human life that was once so busy there, and describe the birds that have taken over the farm now. Frost does not specify the birds until the very end of the poem, when they turn out to be a species

Wyndham Lewis. 1938.

whose spring song, a two-note falling call, leads simple people to
think that they are lamenting. But the poet knows better, and he uses
the particular image to make a general point about nature's indifference
to man's affairs:

> For them there was really nothing sad.
> But though they rejoiced in the nest they kept,
> One had to be versed in country things
> Not to believe the phoebes wept.

Most often, his poems' natural images are simply the stage props
with which Frost illustrates and develops psychological moods. He is
the century's finest lyric poet in English, and his best moody lyrics
express that strangeness in beauty that intrigued Bacon and Baudelaire. *To Earthward* begins as a lovely but conventional evocation
of young love:

> Love at the lips was touch
> As sweet as I could bear;
> And once that seemed too much;
> I lived on air . . .

The reader naturally expects that Frost will go on to speak of the more earthly joys of mature and sensual love. But the poem takes another turn. "I crave the stain of tears," Frost says, and then deepens even that into the most somber of desires:

> When stiff and sore and scarred
> I take away my hand
> From leaning on it hard
> In grass and sand,
>
> The hurt is not enough:
> I long for weight and strength
> To feel the earth as rough
> To all my length.

Poems like this, especially *Stopping by Woods on a Snowy Evening*, go into dark places of the mind, and Frost might have led us further than even Emily Dickinson. But he became popular, and the Victorian fate overtook him: he stopped developing and began to repeat himself, censor himself, and play the sage among his followers. He kept his lyric gift to the end, like the great Victorians who came before him, but he held himself back; as one of his titles puts it, he went "neither out far nor in deep."

That reproach can hardly be made about two other American poets, Ezra Pound (1885–1972) and Thomas Stearns Eliot (1888–1965). Eliot went more deeply into the mind's religious experience of life, and Pound went further out into our complex cultural and ethical inheritance, than any other modern poets. As the widely read young poet Coleridge had discovered and fostered the poetry of Wordsworth, so Pound the literary explorer hovered paternally and professorially over the young Eliot, drumming up financial support and publishers, and giving him freely and unselfishly the advice that, for instance, transformed *The Waste Land* from its original sprawling and unwieldy shape into the terse and elliptical poem it now is. While Yeats (to whom Pound also gave extremely valuable advice) explored the evocativeness of natural symbols, Pound and Eliot explored our conscious cultural heritage, especially in literature.

As an overeducated Harvard student and graduate school dropout, Eliot wandered through a Europe on the brink of World War I, absorbed its cultural malaise and moral decadence, and attempted to strike the pose of the Baudelairean, sophisticated dandy. During the war he settled in England, worked as a bank clerk, married unhappily, and began to move toward a religious sense of life. When he returned to the themes of malaise and decadence in *The Waste Land* (1922), he saw those qualities not as symptoms of a falling off in modern life·but as typical manifestations of religiously and psychologically sick existence throughout history. The perverse and crippled sexuality he at-

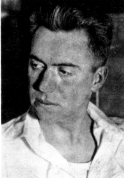

During the 1920s New York's Greenwich Village
—the subject of John Sloan's Wet Night, Washington Square (left)—was the poetic capital of the
country. The bohemian community's denizens
included (clockwise from top): Edna St. Vincent Millay, whose unrestrained verse celebrations of moral freedom were vastly popular in
her day and earned the poet a Pulitzer when she
was only thirty-one; Marianne Moore, acting
editor of The Dial from 1925 to 1929 and practicing poet for decades thereafter. Moore's first
volume of poetry was published without her
knowledge in 1921 by fellow poet Hilda Doo-
little. Other volumes followed at regular inter-
vals, all of them distinguished by a restricted
focus and lapidary polish. Hart Crane, on the
other hand, chose as his subject matter the whole
of modern mechanized society. A powerful if
undisciplined talent, Crane saw his major poetic
work, The Bridge, as an answer to the despairing negativism of Eliot's The Waste Land. E. E.
Cummings, whose penchant for eccentric typo-
graphy has tended to obscure his wit and his
lyric gifts, was in many ways the most independent and individual poet of the entire group.

tributed in the poem to Belladonna, Lil, and the working girls echoes that of Cleopatra, Queen Elizabeth, and Aeneas' mistress Dido. Sin pervades history, and only redemption can save us from it—the redemption evoked in the hyacinth girl, the song of the nightingale, and the possibility of rain. But no rain comes for Tiresias, the multiple protagonist of the poem, and grace came only slowly to its author. Yet by 1935 he had written *Ash Wednesday*, *Journey of the Magi*, and the first of his *Four Quartets*, a major meditation on grace and redemption from sin and error, and the finest of his works.

Meanwhile, his old literary companion had gone a very different route. Like Eliot, Pound had hastily left his backward America for Europe—the two men met in London in 1914—and once there Pound set out to be the greatest energizer of art in the century. Not only did he lavish his talents and interests on Yeats, Eliot, and Frost as well as many others, but he plunged into discussions of painting and sculpture and music, and he generally stirred up the world of art. At the same time, he was slowly bringing his own poetry out of its over-indebtedness to the Provençal troubadours, to Browning and Yeats, and to many other influences, including Oriental verse forms and ideograms. He was working and theorizing toward the writing of his *Cantos*, ultimately more than a hundred poems surveying the history of world culture and constituting a microcosm of it.

Unfortunately, Pound's mind was also busying itself with political, economic, and social theorizing. Much of this was to find confused expression in the *Cantos* and in innumerable books, essays, newspaper articles, and letters; some of it, pushed to extremes by Pound's growing sense of frustration and paranoia, was to eventuate in anti-Semitism and approval of fascism. (Eliot, always more cautious, had abandoned these fashionable Anglo-Saxon attitudes when the fashions changed.) Caught in Italy as World War II broke out, Pound began a series of rambling talks on a Roman radio station, condemning President Roosevelt, supporting Mussolini, lecturing about economics, and generally making a fool of himself. When the American army entered Italy he was arrested, charged with treason, and imprisoned in a stockade outside Pisa, where he wrote some of his finest *Cantos*. He was never brought to trial. Instead, he was confined outside Washington, D. C., in St. Elizabeth's Hospital for the criminally insane until 1958, when his relatives brought him to Italy. He died in Venice in 1972, having for some time preserved an almost complete literary and human silence.

Pound left behind him, especially in the *Cantos*, a legacy that poets will continue to study and imitate for years; and amid their frequent incoherence and unintelligibility, among their languages from Greek to Chinese to all the names, quotations, translations, and imitations, he has left descriptions and images and exhortations capable of moving even the least trained of readers.

Yeats, Pound, Eliot, and Stevens constitute the peaks of a wave of poetry that had swelled into the twentieth century with Mallarmé, Valéry, Rilke, Frost, and Thomas Hardy, and that subsided with such poets as W. H. Auden and Dylan Thomas. Although their successors

Quite simply "the greatest energizer of art in the century," Ezra Pound (lower left) nurtured and shaped the careers of dozens of American writers in the first decades of this century, among them Williams, Yeats, Eliot, and Frost. Pound's own poems, notably the Cantos, *are an often impenetrable survey of the whole of world culture. No such obscurantism darkens the poetry of modern Wales' greatest bard, Dylan Thomas (right), whose works are recognized for their lucidity, lyric power, and heightened imagery.*

have not spoken so widely and loftily about the human condition—not even Allen Ginsberg, Charles Olson, and Federico García Lorca—the level of Western poetry and the quality and originality of individual poets have continued to be strikingly high.

No poet yet has shown us the world in a page of verse or held eternity in a poem; but in his next-to-last canto Pound evokes well the boundless aspiration and the necessary humility of poetry. In that canto he surrounds himself with other poets, expresses his admiration for Jules Laforgue, quotes Dante's line about "the great circle of shade," and then, like Wallace Stevens, goes on to juxtapose the ideal and the real: "The vision of the Madonna/ above the cigar butts/ and over the portal." There, among the poets and their worlds, he sums up the *Cantos*:

> I have brought the great ball of crystal;
> who can lift it?
> Can you enter the great acorn of light?
> But the beauty is not the madness
> Tho' my errors and wrecks lie about me.
> And I am not a demigod,
> I cannot make it cohere.

But if even Pound cannot make our chaotic world coherent, still he can end his life's work by stating simultaneously poetry's fragile inconsequence and its possible magic power:

> A little light, like a rushlight
> to lead back to splendour.

8

New Directions

IN THE PREVIOUS CHAPTER we looked closely at some of the major achievements of modern Western poetry. It now seems proper to consider what was going on elsewhere around the world while our attention was focused upon such undisputed giants of modern poetry as Yeats, Eliot, Stevens, and Pound.

Among the poetic traditions of the West, none rivals the Greek, which—despite nearly four centuries of Turkish oppression—has continued unbroken from Homeric times. In this tradition the myths and poems of classical times are still very much alive, and modern Greek poets draw on them with no sense of artificiality or pedantry. (In fact, Níkos Kazantzákis published a 33,333-line sequel to the *Odyssey* in 1938.) The absorption of the past into the present has been evoked most notably by Constantine Caváfy, an Alexandrian poet in whose verses all of Greek history seems to lurk. His finest successor is George Seféris, who, like so many other poets, has spent much of his life in diplomatic service and whose awareness of history supports a recurrent concern for the fate of Greece caught between the pressures of external and internal totalitarianism. "Though pain is the human lot we are not made men merely to suffer," he says in *An Old Man by the River Bank*, and much of his poetry seeks to go beyond suffering into a lucid awareness that is both sensual and intellectual.

Vergil's and Dante's descendants entered the twentieth century precociously, led by Giuseppe Ungaretti, whose early poems focused upon sequences of images isolated by perception and forming not a literal but an emotional landscape. With the passage and pressure of time these early poems thickened into complexity, but the images retained their characteristic unreality: though never merely surrealistic, they did exist primarily in the mind.

Meanwhile, many other voices were leading Italian verse beyond the somber dryness of Giacomo Leopardi and the flamboyant rhetoric of Gabriele D'Annunzio. In a century of long-lived poets Italy boasts an admirable handful: Umberto Saba, Vincenzo Cardarelli, Eugenio Montale, and Salvatore Quasímodo, all but the last born in the nineteenth century. Quasímodo and Montale, who won Nobel prizes in 1959 and 1975 respectively, present somber views of a decaying society framed in appropriate settings and described with terse vividness.

Along with Ungaretti, these poets constituted the central forces of

Middle-class Americans were offended by the publication, in 1956, of a poem called Howl. *They were equally offended by the poem's author, Allen Ginsberg, the bearded young counterculture hero who reputedly wrote much of the work in question while under the influence of peyote. At a poetry reading in Washington Square Park (opposite) Ginsberg fans and idle curiosity seekers throng to hear the guru-poet recite from his own works.*

hermeticism between the wars. Like futurism, objectivism, vorticism, imagism, and surrealism, this movement appears far less complex and revolutionary in retrospect than its title and early reputation suggest. Basically, all these movements were attempts to stylize and classify modern extensions of poetry beyond the rational, social, and objective voices of the nineteenth century. We read the products of such movements with no great difficulty now: in fact, much that once seemed obscure has become increasingly intelligible with time, and what was intended to evade the reason no longer worries us by doing so. And we see the past continuing even in the experiments—quite explicitly in Quasímodo's *Man of My Time*, but also in Montale's *Little Testament*, a bleak poem whose title comes appropriately and allusively from François Villon.

Of the three major sources of German poetry—Germany, Austria, and Switzerland—two suffered so terribly from war and totalitarianism in this century that the survival of German literature itself is something of a surprise, and it is understandable that much of what is best in it was produced outside Germany and in those tentative times before and after World War I. The best German poet since Goethe was undoubtedly Rainer Maria Rilke. Born in Prague in 1875, he lived in Paris for much of his creative life, traveled extensively, and ended his life in a Swiss tower. While in his thirties Rilke was to develop a deep friendship with the much older French sculptor Auguste Rodin, to whom the poet dedicated a 1908 volume of verse in which central images were evoked and responded to with myth-making intensity. Then came World War I, for Rilke a long period of inwardness, complex visions of isolation and symbolic release, and a final brief period of calm. The poems and poetic series—the *Duino Elegies* and the *Sonnets to Orpheus*—in which Rilke expressed this spiritual progress constitute a poetic achievement that dwarfs the relatively fragmentary works of later German poets. No one since Rilke has been able to combine so many objects of life and thought, and the pressure of history has sent many German poets into mystic vagueness, surrealist obscurity, and the evasiveness of simple satire.

Perhaps the most forceful survivor of these many negative influences was the German doctor Gottfried Benn (1866–1956), whose vision of life characteristically emphasized its physical aspects, presented human ideas and ethics cynically, and—as he put it in perhaps his best poem, *Late*—found no point to existence:

> so many lies beloved,
> so many words believed,
> that only came from the round of the lips,
> and your own heart
> so changeable, bottomless and momentary—

Such cynicism is often found in the poetry—and the prose—of our century, and the events of the past decades encourage us to agree with it all too easily. The result is often a sentimentality of despair, as can be seen in the ending of another Benn poem, *Fragments*:

Níkos Kazantzákis (above) spent twelve long years rewriting and reworking the summation of his life's thought, a massive modern sequel to Homer's Odyssey. When the epic was published in 1938 astonished critics railed against Kazantzákis for daring to tamper with the most sacrosanct of Greek poems. Around the time that Kazantzákis' Odyssey was creating a furor in Greek literary circles, the hermetic school of poetry was thriving in Italy. Led by Eugenio Montale, Giuseppe Ungaretti (right, above), and Salvatore Quasímodo (right, below), this offshoot of the French symbolist movement rejected conventional styles and subject matter in favor of an impressionistic approach and abstruse language.

Crises of expression and bouts of eroticism,
That is the man of today,
His inwardness a vacuum;
The survival of personality
Is preserved by the clothing
Which, where material is good, may last ten years.

The rest fragments,
Half tones,
Snatches of melody from neighbours' houses,
Negro spirituals
Or Ave Marias.

Such generalities as "the man of today" are always suspect; such simple oppositions as hollowness and vague religiosity are not intellectually respectable; and the speaker's viewpoint seems suspiciously above it all, suspiciously like God's. Such are the materials of modern sentimentality —a vice to which another German poet, Bertolt Brecht, was equally prone, although he often leavened the results of his efforts with humor and with a generous measure of Communist positive thinking. As for the rest, modern German poets seem to lack sufficient confidence in their cultural tradition and, perhaps, sufficient distance from their crippling political heritage.

The greatest recent poetic event in Russia was the publication, in 1965, of Anna Akhmatova's last collection of poems, *The Course of Time*. When she died the following year at the age of seventy-seven, her influence was as strong as it had been in her youth and her poetry had found, in the sufferings of her country, a theme worthy of it, a theme on which she speaks even more immediately than Boris Pasternak. For years her "beautiful clarity" and the vivid immediacy of her perceptions had been used to contrive poems out of endless variations on love. "How strange it is that when women—who in real life are so strong and so sensitive to all of love's enchantment—begin to write, all they know," Akhmatova wrote, "is a love that is tormenting, morbidly perceptive, and despairing."

She might have written of such love all her life—a Russian Emily Dickinson—if it had not been for the Communists, who shot her first husband in the 1920s and jailed her second husband and her son repeatedly during the rest of her life. The poems that resulted—especially *Requiem* and *Poem without a Hero*—powerfully connect her personal suffering with that of all Russia. She introduces the former poem with a brief and evocative anecdote. Akhmatova is standing outside the huge Leningrad prison with hundreds of other women when . . .

someone recognized me. Then a woman with lips blue with cold who was standing behind me, and of course had never heard of my name, came out of the numbness that affected us all and whispered in my ear— we all spoke in whispers there:
"Can you describe this?"
I said, "I can!"
Then something resembling a smile slipped over what had once been her face.

Akhmatova's ill-fated younger contemporary Osip Mandelshtam (1891–?1940) is one of the most attractive figures of twentieth-century poetry. Essentially a simple man, in love with poems and domestic life, he saw the Communist takeover of Russia in 1917 as dangerous but otherwise almost irrelevant. Thereafter Mandelshtam seriously attempted to maintain his detachment and live as an individual, but this alone was sufficient to bring down on him governmental hostility and harassment of the sort visited on Akhmatova. An instance of it occurred in 1933 at an unpublicized but crowded public reading of his poetry: an agent provocateur asked him to give his opinion of Soviet poetry and of the older, prerevolutionary poets. "What is it you want of me? What answer?" Mandelshtam replied, recognizing the inescapable trap. "I am the friend of my friends!" he declared. Then, after a momentary pause, he shouted, "I am the contemporary of Akhmatova!" And when, somewhat later, Mandelshtam was so indiscreet as to write a poem about Stalin, the harassment intensified, leading to a series of imprisonments and to his probable death in a prison camp near Vladivostok.

Far and away the best-known poet of Spain in our century is Federico García Lorca (1898–1936), in part because from his tranquil and traditional youth through his confrontation with New York during the Depression to his brutal murder by Falangists during Spain's Civil War, Lorca embodied certain central experiences of modern life. Although his early poems reflect the characteristic Spanish awareness of death, they are essentially folklorist, traditional, and innocent. But in 1929–30 Lorca spent an unsettling year at Columbia University in New York City, learning no English but encountering at its economic worst the century's new materialistic and mechanical civilization. He responded by turning away from his earlier poetic models toward a new artistic sophistication. Close to Rafael Alberti, Salvador Dali, Luis Buñuel and other explorers of surrealism, and interested also in the long visionary poems of Blake and Whitman, Lorca was to fuse his two enthusiasms into a series of poems published after his death as *Poet in New York*. They express a grim sense of the New World, characterized by this passage from *Cry to Rome (From the Chrysler Building Tower)*:

> For see: there is none to apportion the bread and the wine
> or cultivate grass in the mouths of the dead,
> none to turn back the linens of quiet
> or weep for the elephant's wounds.
> Only the blacksmiths,
> a million, to temper the chains for the still-to-be-born.
> Only carpenters,
> a million, to hammer the coffins unmarked by a cross.
> Only a rout of laments,
> undoing their clothing and awaiting the bullet.

Lorca's death was soon followed by that of Antonio Machado, Miguel de Unamuno, César Vallejo, and the promising younger poet Miguel Hernández—all victims of the Spanish Fascists. With their deaths and the consolidation of Franco's power, art could maintain itself in Spain no longer. Juan Ramón Jiménez was to win a Nobel

By refusing to compromise his values or his regard for good poetry, Yevgeny Alexandrovich Yevtushenko (above) has become his generation's unchallenged literary spokesman in the Soviet Union. Chilean poet and militant Communist Pablo Neruda (left), outspoken in his fervent support of the downtrodden masses, has received similar acclaim as an exemplar of Latin-American poetry.

Prize for his lyric, intensely concentrated "pure poetry" in 1956, after years of self-imposed exile; and Pablo Neruda in Chile and Octavio Paz in Mexico became the leading poets in Spanish.

Both Paz and Neruda are associated in the public mind with politics. Neruda (1904–73) spent much of his life serving Chile abroad as a consul in Spain, Mexico, and the Orient; Paz (1914–   ) has served his native land in France and India, and represented Mexico at the United Nations as well. Both were stirred deeply by the Spanish Civil War, but while Paz remained within the conventional political spectrum, Neruda moved increasingly toward the left as Chile moved toward right-wing totalitarianism. In 1953 he accepted the Stalin Prize, the Soviet Union's most prestigious literary award, and except for a brief period at the end of his life, during the Allende regime, Neruda was an exile even in his own country.

Except for his 1954 collection, *The Grapes and the Wind*, there is little that is explicitly political in Neruda's poetry. But for a long period he subordinated his personal sensibility, attempting to speak for and to the masses of mankind, sometimes reporting in drab verse their drab lives and sometimes, as in *The Heights of Machu Picchu*, attempting to evoke myths that would bind everyone together. The resulting works are uneven, perhaps deliberately so, Neruda having opted for what he elsewhere called "the poetry of the impure":

The used surfaces of things, the wear that the hands give to things, the air, tragic at times, pathetic at others, of such things—all lend a curious attractiveness to the reality of the world that should not be underprized. . . . Let that be the poetry we search for . . . a poetry impure as the clothing we wear, or our bodies, soup-stained, soiled with our shameful behavior, our wrinkles and vigils and dreams, observations and prophecies, declarations of loathing and love . . . the shocks of encounter, political loyalties, denials and doubt, affirmations and taxes.

Octavio Paz is more moderate, individual, and delicate than this, about ideas as well as the world. At the end of *Nor Heaven nor Earth*, a poem in which he denounces "carnivorous love," "destructive purity," economic injustice, and human imperfection, Paz steps back to say rather wistfully, "I used to believe in all this." This attractively modest withdrawal from absolute certainty into individual doubt aligns Paz with another kind of poetry now popular in Spanish America—the intellectual, spare, and skeptical analysis represented especially by the noted Argentine writer Jorge Luis Borges. But it is noteworthy that toward the end of his life Neruda, too, moved closer to this kind of poetry, toward a skepticism about values, meanings, and the self.

The French are given to the issuing of manifestos, but the irrational assertions of surrealism—perhaps the most profoundly influential of all modern literary movements—attracted most of the century's major French poets. Guillaume Apollinaire, who named the movement; André Breton, its most dedicated adherent; Jules Supervielle, its best novelist; Pierre Reverdy, Paul Eluard, Louis Aragon, Robert Desnos, René Char —all plunged into surrealism or dabbled at its brink. But surrealism, like many another frail aesthetic notion, shattered against the rocks of painful fact, especially the overwhelming fact of World War II. Eluard, Aragon, Char, and Desnos turned from aesthetes to Resistance heroes, and their poetry turned with them to face the often grim facts of life and the needs of the mind.

Older kinds of French poetry also continued into our own time. The long-winded visionary poetry to which Hugo had turned in his old age was taken up by two Catholic poets, Paul Claudel and Charles Péguy, and by one secular but mythic poet, the diplomat and Nobel Prize winner St. John Perse. The more traditional and regimented French craftsmanship was displayed by the heir of Mallarmé, the wittily rational Paul Valéry (1871–1945), whose poetic voice was that of a hesitant man shut off from life by his intellect. Rilke had imagined a beautifully sculptured Greek torso as telling him, "you must change your life"; Valéry's *Graveyard by the Sea* introduces a characteristically weakening "try": "The wind is rising! . . . One must try to live!" But in Valéry's prose the intellect is at home and assured, and even while the surrealists were having their day in the sun Valéry was defending the old conventions before the French Academy:

> It is in France that the consideration of form, the exigency of form, and preoccupation with form prevail. Neither the force of the ideas, nor the interest provoked by the passions described, nor the marvelous generation of images, nor even a burst of genius, suffice to satisfy a nation so difficult as never fully to enjoy anything that cannot be enjoyed after reflection.

What gives a work this form? Arbitrariness itself, Valéry answers; the organized and decreed arbitrariness of literary rules. "The conventions are arbitrary, or so considered at least; but skepticism is hardly possible in regard to the rules of a game." Such a remark may seem scandalous, he noted, because most people prefer not to think of poetry as a game. But there is value in Valéry's position—which, in fact, was echoed by Robert Frost, a serious poet and a fierce tennis player, when he muttered that writing free verse is like playing tennis without a net.

Modern Oriental poetry is characterized by the continued use of traditional forms, most of them brief, and by the introduction into them of contemporary images and ideas. The result of this attempt to pour new wine into old bottles is usually more curious than artistically successful, as is demonstrated by the poems of Mao Tse-tung. In Japan, to take a more representative case, the traditional *tanka* and *haiku* forms continue to be used, although the poets often speak of modern events and use words new to the poetic language. The Japanese have long made a practice of imitating and assimilating foreign literary forms, and therefore it is hardly surprising that in the postwar period many Japanese poets have written relatively long and unstructured Western-style poems. One reason, of course, is that fifteen centuries of fixed-syllable verse have pretty well covered the ground: the Meiji emperor alone is said to have written more than one hundred thousand *tanka*. The result of such an inundation has been expressed—in *haiku*, of course—by the contemporary Japanese poet Masaoka Shiki:

British-born W. H. Auden (below), regarded in his time as the most prolific and truly intellectual poet writing in English, became an American citizen in 1946. Soon after that his poems began to lose their radical Marxist flavor and become overtly Christian. Unlike Auden, the younger English poet Ted Hughes (bottom) looked beyond the veneer of man's spiritual self, seeking the powerful forces of survival that ultimately bind all living creatures as kindred souls. Less preoccupied with those potentially destructive impulses, the American poet Theodore Roethke (right) was lauded for his precise imagery and vigorous language.

Looking through
Three thousand *haiku*
On two persimmons.

The poetry of no other language has been so influential in our century as that written in English and in England. The interesting thing is that very little of that poetry was written by Englishmen. This sounds paradoxical, and it is. Yeats, Eliot, Pound, and even Frost wrote much of their best poetry while living in England, where they had no major native rivals. It remained for a later generation to produce Dylan Thomas, the expatriates D. H. Lawrence and Robert Graves, and W. H. Auden (1907–73), an excellent lyric poet who later became an American citizen. Auden's works, which celebrate commonplace objects and uncommon events, include this tribute to fellow poet Arthur Rimbaud:

> The nights, the railway-arches, the bad sky,
> His horrible companions did not know it;
> But in that child the rhetorician's lie
> Burst like a pipe: the cold had made a poet.
>
> Drinks bought him by his weak and lyric friend
> His senses systematically deranged,
> To all accustomed nonsense put an end;
> Till he from lyre and weakness was estranged.
>
> Verse was a special illness of the ear;
> Integrity was not enough; that seemed
> The hell of childhood: he must try again.
>
> Now, galloping through Africa, he dreamed
> Of a new self, the son, the engineer,
> His truth acceptable to lying men.

At present there are only two individual and interesting English poets, Philip Larkin and Ted Hughes. Larkin has been able to maintain a conversational tone in seemingly casual but skillful verse, while Hughes—especially through his unpleasant persona Crow—has moved from often dazzling verbal and imagistic dexterity into a consistently bleaker landscape of death.

Samuel Beckett's poetry, though inferior to his prose (and often written now in French), constitutes the only first-rate individual work to survive the crippling influence of Joyce and Yeats upon Irish literature. Thomas McGreevy had some partial success, it is true, and Patrick Kavanagh wrote much competent autobiographical verse, but the past was too much with them; like Theodore Roethke in America, they were never able to establish an individual poetic voice.

It is to America, then, that most poets look nowadays, and what they see there is a vastly overcrowded mass of poets, most of them publishing too often and many all too inclined toward clique and coterie. Earlier in the century, France took the lead in developing extremes in poetry—from the traditional formalities of Perse, Claudel, and

Valéry to the wildest experiments of surrealism and Dada. But now it is in the United States that poets are most willing to try anything—even while poetry in other languages is undergoing a process of homogenization that threatens to make Finns, Germans, Japanese, and Israelis sound like Americans. This is unfortunate, but there is no denying that contemporary American verse offers foreigners a well-stocked supermarket of models from which to choose. Critics and anthologists have labored for years to categorize our nest of singing birds, without much success. Still, some groupings must be made, however irrational, arbitrary, and overlapping.

T. S. Eliot cultivated a poetic voice so distinctive that imitations of it sounded merely plagiaristic, and he moved into a semi-orthodox Christianity that later poets found unpalatable. Yeats was equally individual and unattractive, except to Roethke, and most American poets attempting deliberate newness turned to Pound and his domestic rival William Carlos Williams. Pound's *Cantos* and his theoretical pronouncements provide more material than our century is likely to digest, however, while Williams is simple and homespun. A simplified Pound, a deified Williams, plus Whitman and a dash of Hart Crane, and the radical poets had the makings of their new aesthetic. It began, so far as such matters have a beginning, with Robert Duncan and a few other San Francisco poets in the late 1940s. Soon thereafter Duncan visited the extraordinarily influential Black Mountain College in North Carolina, where he taught with Charles Olson and Robert Creeley and fostered a younger generation of radical poets.

In the late fifties the center of this movement shifted west again. A group of New Yorkers, among them Allen Ginsberg, Jack Kerouac, and Gregory Corso, moved out to join Gary Snyder, Philip Whalen, Lawrence Ferlinghetti, and others in San Francisco, where journalists tagged them with Kerouac's misunderstood label "beat" and publicized them out of all proportion to their achievements. This group's most insistent theoretician was Charles Olson, producer of the sprawling and ambitious *Maximus* poems and self-styled orginator of "projective verse." Its central doctrine may be summarized as follows: In composing, the poet's head chooses the syllables through his ear, his heart chooses the line lengths through his breath, and his perception, through the eye, determines the images that constitute the "field" of his poem. This widely praised formulation indicates the state of education in America, rather than any advance in aesthetics. Much of it had been said before, especially by Pound and Williams, and also by Claudel, who had claimed that his poetic line corresponded to the rhythm of human breathing and the heartbeat.

In practice, projective verse is oral, rhetorical, and highly subjective, with an emphasis on declamatory public performance. Commenting on his best-known early poem, the sensible Ginsberg remarked that, ideally, each line of *Howl* should be a single breath unit, but that when he recorded the poem he had been too tired to manage such long passages in single breaths. Such writing, or spontaneous invention, is at a far remove from Valéry's deliberate composition; Ginsberg describes the making of his *Sunflower Sutra* as "composition time 20 minutes, me

Robert Traill Spence Lowell (above) was the first American poet to write in the intimate, introspective verse style that has since been dubbed "confessional" poetry. This new approach to poetry was to prove the undoing of at least one of Lowell's contemporaries and two of his disciples. The aging author of 77 Dream Songs, *John Berryman (top), along with Sylvia Plath (right, above) and Anne Sexton (right, below), all harboring unresolved personal torments, wrote poems filled with angst and death wishes that were ultimately fulfilled by suicide.*

at desk scribbling, Kerouac at cottage door waiting for me to finish so we could go off somewhere party." The resulting subjectivity became widely popular, if not with all readers then at least with many poets. "I am mainly preoccupied with the world as I experience it," wrote Frank O'Hara. "The rhythms of my poems follow the rhythm of the . . . life I'm leading," said Gary Snyder; Michael McClure aimed at a book that would be "an active part of me of all my feelings and moods and my life"; and Imamu Amiri Baraka (LeRoi Jones) declared that "MY POETRY is whatever I think I am."

Meanwhile, other poets were following more conventional poetic paths. Roethke, John Berryman, and Robert Lowell wrote highly personal poems, sometimes almost confessional in nature, dealing with childhood, family, religion, and mental problems. Lowell was especially remarkable for his compressed intensity—so different from the expansive rhetoric of projective verse—and for his willingness to go deeply into the dark complexities of his psyche. These qualities made him especially attractive to two younger poets, Sylvia Plath and Anne Sexton, who had mental problems of their own. (Sexton has described how she and Plath used to audit Lowell's poetry course at Boston University and then have cocktails at the Copley Plaza and talk about their suicide attempts.) In their later poetry both women exploited this subject, and both committed suicide; but Plath is the better poet, demonstrating remarkable artistic control, compression, and invention, and seasoning her often grim material with a delightful and sane wit.

Although there were many practicing women poets already on the scene—most notably the finely individual Marianne Moore and the transplanted Englishwoman Denise Levertov—it was Plath and Sexton who gave tremendous impetus to what we can now call feminist poetry, a form that takes as its main concern the situation of being female in an often hostile world. It is a narrow area, one in which Adrienne Rich is now most successful and one that perhaps will expand in the future to deal with wider themes and materials.

Individual poets continue to appear and develop, and we might look hastily at two examples. John Ashbery is associated with Kenneth Koch and Frank O'Hara, in part at least because they all began at Harvard and met again in New York. O'Hara specialized in imaginative monologues full of high-camp humor, and Ashbery's early writing was, while less comprehensible, equally imitative of the mind in action; he said he was "trying to record a kind of generalized transcript of what's really going on in our minds all day long." His latest poems are more immediately intelligible, however, and permit us to hear his own personal thinking. Philip Levine, who was born in Michigan, reports events rather than thoughts, though they are often distorted by the feelings generated; he uses language more immediately colloquial than Ashbery's and deals with more violent and painful material.

In short, there are no conclusions to be reached. Poetry has not concluded, nor will it until, moments after the final cataclysm, some dying artist slumps over his scrap of paper in the act of shaping his last perceptions into ordered language. As Wallace Stevens observed: "It can never be satisfied, the mind, never."

CONTEMPORARY AMERICAN POETS

If there is any constant in contemporary American verse it is diversity—and it is that quality as much as any other that is represented in the ensuing anthology. Imamu Amiri Baraka, Nikki Giovanni, June Jordan, and Don L. Lee all speak of what it means to be black in white America, but they speak with very different voices. One recollects the smells of a kitchen on Chicago's South Side, another recalls "the smells of slavery"; one reflects upon a mundane but happy childhood, another escapes into "pure flight, pure fantasy." In a very different vein poets John Berryman, Sylvia Plath, and Anne Sexton confront what the latter calls "the almost unnameable lust"—the desire to destroy oneself. In life each submitted to that desire; in dying each left behind a unique and highly personal poetic legacy. Indeed, the true legacy of contemporary poetry may well be its multiplicity of voices, its wide range of styles, and its seemingly limitless variety of subject matter—a scope so vast that it can be no more than hinted at in the selection of poems that follows.

A. R. Ammons

1926–

From *Selected Poems* by A.R. Ammons. Copyright © 1968 by Cornell University. Reprinted by permission of Cornell University Press.

Visit

It is not far to my place:
you can come smallboat,
pausing under shade in the eddies
   or going ashore
         to rest, regard the leaves

   or talk with birds and
shore weeds: hire a full-grown man not
late in years to oar you
   and choose a canoe-like thin ship;
         (a dumb man is better and no

   costlier; he will attract
the reflections and silences under leaves:)
travel light: a single book, some twine:
   the river is muscled at rapids with trout
         and a laurel limb

   will make a suitable spit: if you
leave in the forenoon, you will arrive
with plenty of light
   the afternoon of the third day: I will
         come down to the landing

   (tell your man to look for it,
the dumb have clear sight and are free of
visions) to greet you with some made
   wine and a special verse:
         or you can come by shore:

   choose the right: there the rocks
cascade less frequently, the grade more gradual:
treat yourself gently: the ascent thins both
   mind and blood and you must
         keep still a dense reserve

   of silence we can poise against
conversation: there is little news:
I found last month a root with shape and
   have heard a new sound among
         the insects: come.

Imamu Amiri Baraka

1934–

From *Preface to a 20-Volume Suicide Note* by LeRoi Jones. Copyright © 1961 by LeRoi Jones. Published by Totem/Corinth Books. Reprinted by permission of the Sterling Lord Agency.

The Turncoat

The steel fibrous slant & ribboned glint
of water. The Sea. Even my secret speech is moist
with it. When I am alone & brooding, locked in

with dull memories & self hate, & the terrible disorder
of a young man.

I move slowly. My cape spread stiff & pressing cautiously
in the first night wind off the Hudson. I glide down
onto my own roof, peering in at the pitiful shadow of myself.

How can it mean anything? The stop & spout, the
wind's dumb shift. Creak of the house & wet smells
coming in. Night forms on my left. The blind still
up to admit a sun that no longer exists. Sea move.

I dream long bays & towers . . . & soft steps on moist sand.
I become them, sometimes. Pure flight. Pure fantasy. Lean.

John Berryman

1914–1972

From *77 Dream Songs* by John
Berryman. Copyright © 1959,
1962, 1963, 1964 by John Berryman. Reprinted by permission of
Farrar, Straus & Giroux, Inc.

Henry's Confession

Nothin very bad happen to me lately.
How you explain that?—I explain that, Mr Bones,
terms o' your bafflin odd sobriety.
Sober as man can get, no girls, no telephones,
what could happen bad to Mr Bones?
—*If* life is a handkerchief sandwich,

in a modesty of death I join my father
who dared so long agone leave me.
A bullet on a concrete stoop
close by a smothering southern sea
spreadeagled on an island, by my knee.
—You is from hunger, Mr Bones,

I offers you this handkerchief, now set
your left foot by my right foot,
shoulder to shoulder, all that jazz,
arm in arm, by the beautiful sea,
hum a little, Mr Bones.
—I saw nobody coming, so I went instead.

Seedy Henry rose up shy in de world
& shaved & swung his barbells, duded Henry up
and p.a.'d poor thousands of persons on topics of grand
moment to Henry, ah to those less & none.
Wif a book of his in either hand
he is stript down to move on.

—Come away, Mr Bones.

—Henry is tired of the winter,
& haircuts, & a squeamish comfy   ruin-prone proud national
          mind,   & Spring (in the city so called).

Henry likes Fall.
He would be prepared to live in a world of Fall
for ever, impenitent Henry.
But the snows and summers grieve & dream;

these fierce & airy occupations, and love,
raved away so many of Henry's years
it is a wonder that, with in each hand
one of his own mad books and all,
ancient fires for eyes, his head full
& his heart full, he's making ready to move on.

Elizabeth Bishop

1911–

A Cold Spring

for Jane Dewey. Maryland

"Nothing is so beautiful as spring."—Hopkins

A cold spring:
the violet was flawed on the lawn.
For two weeks or more the trees hesitated;
the little leaves waited,
carefully indicating their characteristics.
Finally a grave green dust
settled over your big and aimless hills.
One day, in a chill white blast of sunshine,
on the side of one a calf was born.
The mother stopped lowing
and took a long time eating the after-birth,
a wretched flag,
but the calf got up promptly
and seemed inclined to feel gay.

The next day
was much warmer.
Greenish-white dogwood infiltrated the wood,
each petal burned, apparently, by a cigarette-butt;
and the blurred redbud stood
beside it, motionless, but almost more
like movement than any placeable color.
Four deer practised leaping over your fences.
The infant oak-leaves swung through the sober oak.
Song-sparrows were wound up for the summer,
and in the maple the complementary cardinal
cracked a whip, and the sleeper awoke,
stretching miles of green limbs from the south.
In his cap the lilacs whitened,

then one day they fell like snow.
Now, in the evening,
a new moon comes.
The hills grow softer. Tufts of long grass show
where each cow-flop lies.
The bull-frogs are sounding,
slack strings plucked by heavy thumbs.
Beneath the light, against your white front door,
the smallest moths, like Chinese fans,
flatten themselves, silver and silver-gilt
over pale yellow, orange, or gray.
Now, from the thick grass, the fireflies
begin to rise:
up, then down, then up again:
lit on the ascending flight,
drifting simultaneously to the same height,
—exactly like the bubbles in champagne.
—Later on they rise much higher.
And your shadowy pastures will be able to offer
these particular glowing tributes
every evening now throughout the summer.

Robert Bly

1926–

Those Being Eaten by America

The cry of those being eaten by America,
Others pale and soft being stored for later eating

And Jefferson
Who saw hope in new oats

The wild houses go on
With long hair growing from between their toes
The feet at night get up
And run down the long white roads by themselves

The dams reverse themselves and want to go stand alone in the desert

Ministers who dive headfirst into the earth
The pale flesh
Spreading guiltily into new literatures

That is why these poems are so sad
The long dead running over the fields

The mass sinking down
The light in children's faces fading at six or seven

The world will soon break up into small colonies of the saved

Gwendolyn Brooks

1917–

The Chicago Picasso

August 15, 1967

> "Mayor Daley tugged a white ribbon, loosing the blue percale wrap. A hearty cheer went up as the covering slipped off the big steel sculpture that looks at once like a bird and a woman."
> —Chicago *Sun-Times*

(Seiji Ozawa leads the Symphony.
The Mayor smiles.
And 50,000 See.)

Does man love Art? Man visits Art, but squirms.
Art hurts. Art urges voyages—
and it is easier to stay at home,
the nice beer ready.
    In commonrooms
we belch, or sniff, or scratch.
Are raw.

But we must cook ourselves and style ourselves for Art, who
is a requiring courtesan.
We squirm.
We do not hug the Mona Lisa.
We
may touch or tolerate
an astounding fountain, or a horse-and-rider.
At most, another Lion.

Observe the tall cold of a Flower
which is as innocent and as guilty,
as meaningful and as meaningless as any
other flower in the western field.

Allen Ginsberg

1926–

Sunflower Sutra

I walked on the banks of the tincan banana dock and sat down
    under the huge shade of a Southern Pacific locomotive to
    look at the sunset over the box house hills and cry.
Jack Kerouac sat beside me on a busted rusty iron pole, compan-
    ion, we thought the same thoughts of the soul, bleak and
    blue and sad-eyed, surrounded by the gnarled steel roots
    of trees of machinery.
The oily water on the river mirrored the red sky, sun sank on top
    of final Frisco peaks, no fish in that stream, no hermit in
    those mounts, just ourselves rheumy-eyed and hungover
    like old bums on the riverbank, tired and wily.
Look at the Sunflower, he said, there was a dead gray shadow

against the sky, big as a man, sitting dry on top of a pile of
   ancient sawdust—
— I rushed up enchanted — it was my first sunflower, memories
   of Blake — my visions — Harlem
and Hells of the Eastern rivers, bridges clanking, Joes Greasy
   Sandwiches, dead baby carriages, black treadless tires
   forgotten and unretreaded, the poem of the riverbank,
   condoms & pots, steel knives, nothing stainless, only the
   dank muck and the razor sharp artifacts passing into the
   past —
and the gray Sunflower poised against the sunset, crackly bleak
   and dusty with the smut and smog and smoke of olden
   locomotives in its eye —
corolla of bleary spikes pushed down and broken like a battered
   crown, seeds fallen out of its face, soon-to-be-toothless
   mouth of sunny air, sunrays obliterated on its hairy head
   like a dried wire spiderweb,
leaves stuck out like arms out of the stem, gestures from the
   sawdust root, broke pieces of plaster fallen out of the black
   twigs, a dead fly in its ear,
Unholy battered old thing you were, my sunflower O my soul,
   I loved you then!
The grime was no man's grime but death and human locomotives,
all that dress of dust, that veil of darkened railroad skin, that
   smog of cheek, that eyelid of black mis'ry, that sooty hand
   or phallus or protuberance of artificial worse-than-dirt —
   industrial — modern — all that civilization spotting your
   crazy golden crown —
and those blear thoughts of death and dusty loveless eyes and ends
   and withered roots below, in the home-pile of sand and
   sawdust, rubber dollar bills, skin of machinery, the guts and
   innards of the weeping coughing car, the empty lonely
   tincans with their rusty tongues alack, what more could I
   name, the smoked ashes of some cock cigar, the cunts of
   wheelbarrows and the milky breasts of cars, wornout asses
   out of chairs & sphincters of dynamos—all these
entangled in your mummied roots—and you there standing before
   me in the sunset, all your glory in your form!
A perfect beauty of a sunflower! a perfect excellent lovely
   sunflower existence! a sweet natural eye to the new hip
   moon, woke up alive and excited grasping in the sunset
   shadow sunrise golden monthly breeze!
How many flies buzzed round you innocent of your grime, while
   you cursed the heavens of the railroad and your flower
   soul?
Poor dead flower? when did you forget you were a flower? when
   did you look at your skin and decide you were an impotent
   dirty old locomotive? the ghost of a locomotive? the
   specter and shade of a once powerful mad American
   locomotive?
You were never no locomotive, Sunflower, you were a sunflower!
And you Locomotive, you are a locomotive, forget me not!

So I grabbed up the skeleton thick sunflower and stuck it at my
    side like a scepter,
and deliver my sermon to my soul, and Jack's soul too, and any-
    one who'll listen,
—We're not our skin of grime, we're not our dread bleak dusty
    imageless locomotive, we're all beautiful golden sunflowers
    inside, we're blessed by our own seed & golden hairy naked
    accomplishment-bodies growing into mad black formal
    sunflowers in the sunset, spied on by our eyes under the
    shadow of the mad locomotive riverbank sunset Frisco hilly
    tincan evening sitdown vision.

Nikki Giovanni

1943–

From *Black Feeling, Black Talk,
Black Judgement* by Nikki Giovanni.
Copyright © 1968, 1970 by Nikki
Giovanni. Reprinted by permission of
William Morrow & Company, Inc.

Nikki-Rosa

childhood remembrances are always a drag
if you're Black
you always remember things like living in Woodlawn
with no inside toilet
and if you become famous or something
they never talk about how happy you were to have
your mother
all to yourself and
how good the water felt when you got your bath
from one of those
big tubs that folk in chicago barbecue in
and somehow when you talk about home
it never gets across how much you
understood their feelings
as the whole family attended meetings about Hollydale
and even though you remember
your biographers never understand
your father's pain as he sells his stock
and another dream goes
And though you're poor it isn't poverty that
concerns you
and though they fought a lot
it isn't your father's drinking that makes any difference
but only that everybody is together and you
and your sister have happy birthdays and very good
Christmasses
and I really hope no white person ever has cause
to write about me
because they never understand
Black love is Black wealth and they'll
probably talk about my hard childhood
and never understand that
all the while I was quite happy

John Hollander

1929–

The Night Mirror

What it showed was always the same—
A vertical panel with him in it,
Being a horrible bit of movement
At the edge of knowledge, overhanging
The canyons of nightmare. And when the last
Glimpse was enough—his grandmother,
Say, with a blood-red face, rising
From her Windsor chair in the warm lamplight
To tell him something—he would scramble up,
Waiting to hear himself shrieking, and gain
The ledge of the world, his bed, lit by
The pale rectangle of window, eclipsed
By a dark shape, but a shape that moved
And saw and knew and mistook its reflection
In the tall panel on the closet door
For itself. The silver corona of moonlight
That gloried his glimpsed head was enough
To send him back into silences (choosing
Fear in those chasms below), to reject
Freedom of wakeful seeing, believing
And feeling, for peace and the bondage to horrors
Welling up only from deep within
That dark planet head, spinning beyond
The rim of the night mirror's range, huge
And cold, on the pillow's dark side.

Randall Jarrell

1914–1965

The Woman at the Washington Zoo

The saris go by me from the embassies.

Cloth from the moon. Cloth from another planet.
They look back at the leopard like the leopard.

And I. . . .
                this print of mine, that has kept its color
Alive through so many cleanings; this dull null
Navy I wear to work, and wear from work, and so
To my bed, so to my grave, with no
Complaints, no comment: neither from my chief,
The Deputy Chief Assistant, nor his chief—
Only I complain. . . . this serviceable
Body that no sunlight dyes, no hand suffuses
But, dome-shadowed, withering among columns,

Wavy beneath fountains—small, far-off, shining
In the eyes of animals, these beings trapped
As I am trapped but not, themselves, the trap,
Aging, but without knowledge of their age,
Kept safe here, knowing not of death, for death—
Oh, bars of my own body, open, open!

The world goes by my cage and never sees me.
And there come not to me, as come to these,
The wild beasts, sparrows pecking the llamas' grain,
Pigeons settling on the bears' bread, buzzards
Tearing the meat the flies have clouded. . . .
                                        Vulture,
When you come for the white rat that the foxes left,
Take off the red helmet of your head, the black
Wings that have shadowed me, and step to me as man:
The wild brother at whose feet the white wolves fawn,
To whose hand of power the great lioness
Stalks, purring. . . .
                        You know what I was,
You see what I am: change me, change me!

June Jordan

1936–

From *Some Changes* by June Jordan. Copyright © 1967, 1971 by June Meyer Jordan. Reprinted by permission of E.P. Dutton & Company, Inc.

Poem for My Family:
Hazel Griffin and Victor Hernandez Cruz

Dedicated to Robert Penn Warren

I

December 15, 1811
a black, well-butchered slave
named George took leave of Old Kentucky—true
he left that living hell in pieces—
first his feet fell to the fire
and the jelly of his eyes lay smoking
on the pyre a long while—
but he burned complete
at last he left at least he got away.
The others had to stay there
where he died like meat
(that slave)

how did he live?

                    December 15, 1811

Lilburn Lewis and his brother
cut and killed somebody real
because they missed their mother:

Thomas Jefferson's sweet sister Lucy
Correction: Killed no body: killed a slave
the time was close to Christmas sent the poor
black bastard to the snow zones of a blue-eyed
heaven and he went the way he came like meat
not good enough to eat
not nice enough to see
not light enough to live
he came the way he went like meat.

POEM FOR 175 Pounds
("Poor George")

II

Southern Kentucky, Memphis, New Orleans,
Little Rock, Milwaukee, Brooklyn, San Antonio,
Chicago, Augusta.
I am screaming
do you hear the pulse
destroying properties
of your defense against me and my life
now what are you counting
                              dollar bills or lives?
How did you put me down
as property?
as life?
How did you describe the damage?
I am naked
I am Harlem and Detroit
currently knives and bullets
I am lives
YOUR PROPERTY IS DYING
I am lives
MY LIFE IS BEING BORN
This is a lesson
in American History
What can you teach me?
The fire smells of slavery.

III

Here is my voice the speed and the wondering
darkness of my desire is
all that I am here
all that you never allowed:
I came and went like meat not good enough to eat
remember no remember
yes remember me
the shadow following your dreams
the human sound that never reached your ears
that disappear
vestigial
when the question is my scream

and I am screaming
whiteman
do you hear the loud
the blood, the real hysteria of birth
my life is being born
your property is dying

IV

What can you seize
from the furnace
what can you save?
America
I mean America how
do you intend to incinerate
my slavery?
I have taken my eyes from the light of your fires.
The begging body grows cold.
I see.
I see my self
Alive
A life

Galway Kinnell

1927–

From *What a Kingdom It Was* by
Galway Kinnell. Copyright © 1960
by Galway Kinnell. Reprinted by
permission of Houghton Mifflin Co.

Duck-chasing

I spied a very small brown duck
Riding the swells of the sea
Like a rocking-chair. "Little duck!"
I cried. It paddled away,
I paddled after it. When it dived,
Down I dived: too smoky was the sea,
We were lost. It surfaced
In the west, I torpedoed west
And when it dived I dived,
And we were lost and lost and lost
In the slant smoke of the sea.
When I came floating up on it
From the side, like a deadman,
And yelled suddenly, it took off,
It skimmed the swells as it ascended,
Brown wings burning and flashing
In the sun as the sea it rose over
Burned and flashed underneath it.
I did not see the little duck again.
Duck-chasing is a game like any game.
When it is over it is all over.

Carolyn Kizer

1925–

From *Midnight Was My Cry* by Carolyn Kizer. Copyright © 1961 by Indiana University Press. Reprinted by permission of Doubleday & Company, Inc.

The Great Blue Heron

M. A. K., September, 1880   September, 1955

As I wandered on the beach
I saw the heron standing
Sunk in the tattered wings
He wore as a hunchback's coat.
Shadow without a shadow,
Hung on invisible wires
From the top of a canvas day,
What scissors cut him out?
Superimposed on a poster
Of summer by the strand
Of a long-decayed resort,
Poised in the dusty light
Some fifteen summers ago;
I wondered, an empty child,
"Heron, whose ghost are you?"

I stood on the beach alone,
In the sudden chill of the burned.
My thought raced up the path.
Pursuing it, I ran
To my mother in the house
And led her to the scene.
The spectral bird was gone.
But her quick eye saw him drifting
Over the highest pines
On vast, unmoving wings.
Could they be those ashen things,
So grounded, unwieldy, ragged,

A pair of broken arms
That were not made for flight?
In the middle of my loss
I realized she knew:
My mother knew what he was.

O great blue heron, now
That the summer house has burned
So many rockets ago,
So many smokes and fires
And beach-lights and water-glow
Reflecting pin-wheel and flare:
The old logs hauled away,
The pines and driftwood cleared
From that bare strip of shore
Where dozens of children play;
Now there is only you
Heavy upon my eye.
Why have you followed me here,
Heavy and far away?
You have stood there patiently
For fifteen summers and snows,
Denser than my repose,
Bleaker than any dream,
Waiting upon the day
When, like gray smoke, a vapor
Floating into the sky,
A handful of paper ashes,
My mother would drift away.

Don L. Lee

1942–

From *We Walk the Way of the New World*. Copyright © 1970 by Don L. Lee. Reprinted by permission of Broadside Press.

Big Momma

finally retired   pensionless
from cleaning somebody else's house
she remained home to clean
the one she didn't own.

in her kitchen where we often talked
the *chicago tribune* served as a tablecloth
for the two cups of tomato soup that went
along with my weekly visit & talkingto.

she was in a seriously-funny mood
& from the get-go she was down, realdown;

  roaches around here are like
  letters on a newspaper
  or
  u gonta be a writer, hunh
  when u gone write me some writen
  or
  the way niggers act around here
  if talk cd kill we'd all be dead.

she's somewhat confused about all this *blackness*
but said that it's good when negroes start putting themselves
first and added: we've always shopped at the colored stores,
    & the way niggers cut each other up round here
     every weekend that whiteman don't haveta
    worry bout no revolution specially when he's
     gonta
    haveta pay for it too, anyhow all he's gotta do is
     drop a truck load of *dope* out there
    on 43rd st. & all the niggers & yr revolutionaries
    be too busy getten high & then they'll turn round
    and fight each other over who got the mostest.

we finished our soup and i moved to excuse myself,
as we walked to the front door she made a last comment:
  now *luther* i knows you done changed a lots but if you can
  think back, we never did eat too much pork round here
  anyways, it was bad for the belly.
i shared her smile and agreed.

touching the snow lightly i headed for 43rd st.
at the corner i saw a brother crying while
trying to hold up a lamp post,
thru his watery eyes i cd see big momma's words.
  at sixty-eight
  she moves freely, is often right
  and when there is food
  eats joyously with her own
  real teeth.

Denise Levertov

1923–

From *The Sorrow Dance* by Denise Levertov. Copyright © 1966 by Denise Levertov Goodman. Reprinted by permission of New Directions Publishing Corporation.

What Were They Like?

1) Did the people of Viet Nam
  use lanterns of stone?
2) Did they hold ceremonies
  to reverence the opening of buds?
3) Were they inclined to quiet laughter?

4) Did they use bone and ivory,
   jade and silver, for ornament?
5) Had they an epic poem?
6) Did they distinguish between speech and singing?

1) Sir, their light hearts turned to stone.
   It is not remembered whether in gardens
   stone lanterns illumined pleasant ways.
2) Perhaps they gathered once to delight in blossom,
   but after the children were killed
   there were no more buds.
3) Sir, laughter is bitter to the burned mouth.
4) A dream ago, perhaps. Ornament is for joy.
   All the bones were charred.
5) It is not remembered. Remember,
   most were peasants; their life
   was in rice and bamboo.
   When peaceful clouds were reflected in the paddies
   and the water buffalo stepped surely along terraces,
   maybe fathers told their sons old tales.
   When bombs smashed those mirrors
   there was time only to scream.
6) There is an echo yet
   of their speech which was like a song.
   It was reported their singing resembled
   the flight of moths in moonlight.
   Who can say? It is silent now.

Philip Levine

1928–

From *Not This Pig* by Philip
Levine. Copyright © 1966 by
Philip Levine. Reprinted by per-
mission of Wesleyan University
Press. This poem first appeared
in *The New Yorker*.

The Cemetery at Academy, California

I came here with a young girl
once who perched barefoot on her
family marker. "I will go
here," she said, "next to my sister."
It was early morning and
cold, and I wandered over
the pale clodded ground looking
for something rich or touching.
"It's all wildflowers in the spring,"
she had said, but in July
there were only the curled cut
flowers and the headstones blanked
   out
on the sun side, and the long
shadows deep as oil. I walked

to the sagging wire fence
that marked the margin of the
place and saw where the same
   ground,
festered here and there with reedy
grass, rose to a small knoll
and beyond where a windmill
held itself against the breeze.
I thought I heard her singing on
the stone under the great oak,
but when I got there she was
silent and I wasn't sure
and was ashamed to ask her,
ashamed that I had come here
where her people turned the earth.

Yet I came again, alone,
in the evening when the leaves
turned in the heat toward darkness
so late in coming. There was
her sister, there was her place
undisturbed, and relatives and
friends, and other families
spread along the crests of this
burned hill. When I kneeled
to touch the ground it seemed like
something I had never seen,
the way the pale lumps broke down
to almost nothing, nothing
but the source of what they called

their living. She, younger now
than I, would be here someday
beneath the ground my hand
    combed.
The first night wind caught the
    leaves
above, crackling, and on
the trunk a salamander
faded in the fading light.
One comes for answers to a
place like this and finds even
in the darkness, even in
the sudden flooding of the
headlights, that in time one comes
to be a stranger to nothing.

Robert Lowell

1917–

From *For the Union Dead* by
Robert Lowell. Copyright © 1960
by Robert Lowell. Reprinted by
permission of Farrar, Straus &
Giroux, Inc.

For the Union Dead

"Relinquunt Omnia Servare Rem Publicam."

The old South Boston Aquarium stands
in a Sahara of snow now. Its broken windows are boarded.
The bronze weathervane cod has lost half its scales.
The airy tanks are dry.

Once my nose crawled like a snail on the glass;
my hand tingled
to burst the bubbles
drifting from the noses of the cowed, compliant fish.

My hand draws back. I often sigh still
for the dark downward and vegetating kingdom
of the fish and reptile. One morning last March,
I pressed against the new barbed and galvanized

fence on the Boston Common. Behind their cage,
yellow dinosaur steamshovels were grunting
as they cropped up tons of mush and grass
to gouge their underworld garage.

Parking spaces luxuriate like civic
sandpiles in the heart of Boston.
A girdle of orange, Puritan-pumpkin colored girders
braces the tingling Statehouse,

shaking over the excavations, as it faces Colonel Shaw
and his bell-cheeked Negro infantry
on St. Gaudens' shaking Civil War relief,
propped by a plank splint against the garage's earthquake.

Two months after marching through Boston,
half the regiment was dead;
at the dedication,
William James could almost hear the bronze Negroes breathe.

Their monument sticks like a fishbone
in the city's throat.
Its Colonel is as lean
as a compass-needle.

He has an angry wrenlike vigilance,
a greyhound's gentle tautness;
he seems to wince at pleasure,
and suffocate for privacy.

He is out of bounds now. He rejoices in man's lovely,
peculiar power to choose life and die—
when he leads his black soldiers to death,
he cannot bend his back.

On a thousand small town New England greens,
the old white churches hold their air
of sparse, sincere rebellion; frayed flags
quilt the graveyards of the Grand Army of the Republic.

The stone statues of the abstract Union Soldier
grow slimmer and younger each year—
wasp-wasted, they doze over muskets
and muse through their sideburns . . .

Shaw's father wanted no monument
except the ditch,
where his son's body was thrown
and lost with his "niggers."

The ditch is nearer.
There are no statues for the last war here;
on Boyleston Street, a commercial photograph
shows Hiroshima boiling

over a Mosler Safe, the "Rock of Ages"
that survived the blast. Space is nearer.
When I crouch to my television set,
the drained faces of Negro school-children rise like balloons.

Colonel Shaw
is riding on his bubble,
he waits
for the blesséd break.

The Aquarium is gone. Everywhere,
giant finned cars nose forward like fish;
a savage servility
slides by on grease.

Howard Nemerov
1920–

The Dependencies

This morning, between two branches of a tree
Beside the door, epeira once again
Has spun and signed his tapestry and trap.
I test his early-warning system and
It works, he scrambles forth in sable with
The yellow hieroglyph that no one knows
The meaning of. And I remember now
How yesterday at dusk the nighthawks came
Back as they do about this time each year,
Gray squadrons with the slashes white on wings
Cruising for bugs beneath the bellied cloud.
Now soon the monarchs will be drifting south,
And then the geese will go, and then one day
The little garden birds will not be here.
See how many leaves already have
Withered and turned; a few have fallen, too.
Change is continuous on the seamless web,
Yet moments come like this one, when you feel
Upon your heart a signal to attend
The definite announcement of an end
Where one thing ceases and another starts;
When like the spider waiting on the web
You know the intricate dependencies
Spreading in secret through the fabric vast
Of heaven and earth, sending their messages
Ciphered in chemistry to all the kinds,
The whisper in the bloodstream: it is time.

Frank O'Hara
1926–1966

A Step Away from Them

It's my lunch hour, so I go
for a walk among the hum-colored
cabs. First, down the sidewalk
where laborers feed their dirty
glistening torsos sandwiches
and Coca-Cola, with yellow helmets
on. They protect them from falling
bricks, I guess. Then onto the
avenue where skirts are flipping
above heels and blow up over
grates. The sun is hot, but the
cabs stir up the air. I look
at bargains in wristwatches. There
are cats playing in sawdust.

On
to Times Square, where the sign
blows smoke over my head, and higher
the waterfall pours lightly. A
Negro stands in a doorway with a
toothpick, languorously agitating.
A blonde chorus girl clicks: he
smiles and rubs his chin. Everything
suddenly honks: it is 12:40 of
a Thursday.

Neon in daylight is a
great pleasure, as Edwin Denby would
write, as are light bulbs in daylight.
I stop for a cheeseburger at JULIET'S

CORNER. Giulietta Masina, wife of
Federico Fellini, *e bell' attrice*.
And chocolate malted. A lady in
foxes on such a day puts her poodle
in a cab.

      There are several Puerto
Ricans on the avenue today, which
makes it beautiful and warm. First
Bunny died, then John Latouche,
then Jackson Pollock. But is the

earth as full as life was full, of them?
And one has eaten and one walks,
past the magazines with nudes
and the posters for BULLFIGHT and
the Manhattan Storage Warehouse,
which they'll soon tear down. I
used to think they had the Armory
Show there.

      A glass of papaya juice
and back to work. My heart is in my
pocket, it is Poems by Pierre Reverdy.

Marge Piercy

1936–

From *To Be Of Use* by Marge
Piercy. Copyright © 1972 by
Marge Piercy. Reprinted by permission of Doubleday & Company, Inc.

Councils

We must sit down
and reason together.
We must sit down:
men standing want to hold forth.
They rain down upon bowed heads
and faces lifted.
We must sit down on the floor
on the ground
on the earth
on stones and mats and blankets.
There must be no front to the speaking
no platform, no rostrum,
no stage or table.
We will not crane
to see who is speaking.
Perhaps we should sit in the dark.
In the dark we could utter our feelings.
In the dark we could propose
and describe and suggest.
In the dark we could not see who speaks
and only the words
would say what we think they say.
No one would speak more than twice.
No one would speak less than once.
Thus saying what we feel and what we want,
what we fear for ourselves and each other
into the dark, perhaps we could begin
to begin to listen.
Perhaps we should talk in groups
the size of new families,
not more, never more than twenty.
Perhaps we should start by speaking softly.

The women must learn to dare to speak.
The men must learn to bother to listen.
The women must learn to say I think this is so.
The men must learn to stop dancing solos on the ceiling.
After each speaks, he or she
shall say a ritual phrase:
It is not I who speak but the wind.
Wind blows through me.
Long after me, is the wind.

Sylvia Plath

1932–1963

Daddy

You do not do, you do not do
Any more, black shoe
In which I have lived like a foot
For thirty years, poor and white,
Barely daring to breathe or Achoo.

Daddy, I have had to kill you.
You died before I had time—
Marble-heavy, a bag full of God,
Ghastly statue with one grey toe
Big as a Frisco seal

And a head in the freakish Atlantic
Where it pours bean green over blue
In the waters off beautiful Nauset.
I used to pray to recover you.
Ach, du.

In the German tongue, in the Polish
town
Scraped flat by the roller
Of wars, wars, wars.
But the name of the town is common.
My Polack friend

Says there are a dozen or two.
So I never could tell where you
Put your foot, your root,
I never could talk to you.
The tongue stuck in my jaw.

It stuck in a barb wire snare.
Ich, ich, ich, ich,
I could hardly speak.
I thought every German was you.
And the language obscene

An engine, an engine
Chuffing me off like a Jew.
A Jew to Dachau, Auschwitz, Belsen.
I began to talk like a Jew.
I think I may well be a Jew.

The snows of the Tyrol, the clear
beer of Vienna
Are not very pure or true.
With my gypsy ancestress and my
weird luck
And my Taroc pack and my Taroc
pack
I may be a bit of a Jew.

I have always been scared of *you*,
With your Luftwaffe, your
gobbledygoo.
And your neat moustache
And your Aryan eye, bright blue.
Panzer-man, panzer-man, O You—

Not God but a swastika
So black no sky could squeak
through.
Every woman adores a Fascist,
The boot in the face, the brute
Brute heart of a brute like you.

You stand at the blackboard, daddy,
In the picture I have of you,
A cleft in your chin instead of your
foot
But no less a devil for that, no not
Any less the black man who

172

Bit my pretty red heart in two.
I was ten when they buried you.
At twenty I tried to die
And get back, back, back to you.
I thought even the bones would do.

But they pulled me out of the sack,
And they stuck me together with
      glue.
And then I knew what to do.
I made a model of you,
A man in black with a Meinkampf
      look

And a love of the rack and the screw.
And I said I do, I do.
So daddy, I'm finally through.

The black telephone's off at the root,
The voices just can't worm through.

If I've killed one man, I've killed
      two—
The vampire who said he was you
And drank my blood for a year,
Seven years, if you want to know.
Daddy, you can lie back now.

There's a stake in your fat black heart
And the villagers never liked you.
They are dancing and stamping on
      you.
They always *knew* it was you.
Daddy, daddy, you bastard, I'm
      through.

Adrienne Rich

1929–

From *Poems, Selected and New, 1950–1974* by Adrienne Rich. Copyright © 1975, 1973, 1971, 1969, 1966 by W.W. Norton & Company, Inc. Copyright © 1967, 1963, 1962, 1961, 1960, 1959, 1958, 1957, 1956, 1955, 1954, 1953, 1952, 1951 by Adrienne Rich. Reprinted by permission of W.W. Norton & Company, Inc.

Living in Sin

She had thought the studio would keep itself;
No dust upon the furniture of love.
Half heresy, to wish the taps less vocal,
The panes relieved of grime. A plate of pears,
A piano with a Persian shawl, a cat
Stalking the picturesque amusing mouse
Had been her vision when he pleaded "Come."
Not that at five each separate stair would writhe
Under the milkman's tramp; that morning light
So coldly would delineate the scraps
Of last night's cheese and blank sepulchral bottles;
That on the kitchen shelf among the saucers
A pair of beetle-eyes would fix her own—
Envoy from some black village in the mouldings . . .
Meanwhile her night's companion, with a yawn
Sounded a dozen notes upon the keyboard,
Declared it out of tune, inspected whistling
A twelve hours' beard, went out for cigarettes;
While she, contending with a woman's demons,
Pulled back the sheets and made the bed and found
A fallen towel to dust the table-top,
And wondered how it was a man could wake
From night to day and take the day for granted.
By evening she was back in love again,
Though not so wholly but throughout the night
She woke sometimes to feel the daylight coming
Like a relentless milkman up the stairs.

Theodore Roethke

1908–1963

The Waking

I wake to sleep, and take my waking slow.
I feel my fate in what I cannot fear.
I learn by going where I have to go.

We think by feeling. What is there to know?
I hear my being dance from ear to ear.
I wake to sleep, and take my waking slow.

Of those so close beside me, which are you?
God bless the Ground! I shall walk softly there,
And learn by going where I have to go.

Light takes the Tree; but who can tell us how?
The lowly worm climbs up a winding stair;
I wake to sleep, and take my waking slow.

Great Nature has another thing to do
To you and me; so take the lively air,
And, lovely, learn by going where to go.

This shaking keeps me steady. I should know.
What falls away is always. And is near.
I wake to sleep, and take my waking slow.
I learn by going where I have to go.

Muriel Rukeyser

1913–

Don Baty, the draft resister

I Muriel stood at the altar-table
The young man Don Baty stood with us
I Muriel fell away in me
in dread but in a welcoming
I am Don Baty then I said
before the blue-coated police
ever entered and took him.

I am Don Baty, say we all
we eat our bread, we drink our wine.
Our heritage has come, we know,
your arrest is mine. Yes.
Beethoven saying Amen Amen Amen Amen Amen
and all a singing, earth and eyes,
strong and weaponless.

There is a pounding at the door;
now we bring our lives entire.
I am Don Baty. My dear, my dear,

in a kind of welcoming,
here we meet, here we bring
ourselves. They pound on the wall of time.
The newborn are with us singing.

Anne Sexton

1928–1974

Wanting to Die

Since you ask, most days I cannot remember.
I walk in my clothing, unmarked by that voyage.
Then the almost unnameable lust returns.

Even then I have nothing against life.
I know well the grass blades you mention,
the furniture you have placed under the sun.

But suicides have a special language.
Like carpenters they want to know *which tools*.
They never ask *why build*.

Twice I have so simply declared myself,
have possessed the enemy, eaten the enemy,
have taken on his craft, his magic.

In this way, heavy and thoughtful,
warmer than oil or water,
I have rested, drooling at the mouth-hole.

I did not think of my body at needle point.
Even the cornea and the leftover urine were gone.
Suicides have already betrayed the body.

Still-born, they don't always die,
but dazzled, they can't forget a drug so sweet
that even children would look on and smile.

To thrust all that life under your tongue!—
that, all by itself, becomes a passion.
Death's a sad bone; bruised, you'd say,

and yet she waits for me, year after year,
to so delicately undo an old wound,
to empty my breath from its bad prison.

Balanced there, suicides sometimes meet,
raging at the fruit, a pumped-up moon,
leaving the bread they mistook for a kiss,

leaving the page of the book carelessly open,
something unsaid, the phone off the hook
and the love, whatever it was, an infection.

W. D. Snodgrass

1926–

The Campus on the Hill

Up the reputable walks of old established trees
They stalk, children of the *nouveaux riches;* chimes
Of the tall Clock Tower drench their heads in blessing:
"I don't wanna play at your house;
I don't like you any more."
My house stands opposite, on the other hill,
Among meadows, with the orchard fences down and falling;
Deer come almost to the door.
You cannot see it, even in this clearest morning.
White birds hang in the air between
Over the garbage landfill and those homes thereto adjacent,
Hovering slowly, turning, settling down
Like the flakes sifting imperceptibly onto the little town
In a waterball of glass.
And yet, this morning, beyond this quiet scene,
The floating birds, the backyards of the poor,
Beyond the shopping plaza, the dead canal, the hillside
        lying tilted in the air,
Tomorrow has broken out today:
Riot in Algeria, in Cyprus, in Alabama;
Aged in wrong, the empires are declining,
And China gathers, soundlessly, like evidence.
What shall I say to the young on such a morning?—
Mind is the one salvation?—also grammar?—
No; my little ones lean not toward revolt. They
Are the Whites, the vaguely furiously driven, who resist
Their souls with such passivity
As would make Quakers swear. All day, dear Lord, all day
They wear their godhead lightly.
They look out from their hill and say,
To themselves, "We have nowhere to go but down;
The great destination is to stay."
Surely the nations will be reasonable;
They look at the world—don't they?—the world's way?
The clock just now has nothing more to say.

Gary Snyder

1930–

Milton by Firelight

Piute Creek, August 1955
"Oh hell, what do mine eyes
    with grief behold?"
Working with an old
Singlejack miner, who can sense
The vein and cleavage
In the very guts of rock, can

Blast granite, build
Switchbacks that last for years
Under the beat of snow, thaw,
    mule-hooves.
What use, Milton, a silly story
Of our lost general parents,
    eaters of fruit?

The Indian, the chainsaw boy,
And a string of six mules
Came riding down to camp
Hungry for tomatoes and green
    apples.
Sleeping in saddle-blankets
Under a bright night-sky
Han River slantwise by morning,
Jays squall
Coffee boils

In ten thousand years the Sierras
Will be dry and dead, home of
    the scorpion.

Ice-scratched slabs and bent trees.
No paradise, no fall,
Only the weathering land
The wheeling sky,
Man, with his Satan
Scouring the chaos of the mind.
Oh Hell!
Fire down
Too dark to read, miles from a road
The bell-mare clangs in the meadow
That packed dirt for a fill-in
Scrambling through loose rocks
On an old trail
All of a summer's day.

May Swenson

1919–

From *To Mix With Time* by May
Swenson. Copyright © 1963 by
May Swenson. Reprinted by per-
mission of the author.

✕ Question

Body my house
my horse my hound
what will I do
when you are fallen

Where will I sleep
How will I ride
What will I hunt

Where can I go
without my mount
all eager and quick
How will I know
in thicket ahead
is danger or treasure
when Body my good
bright dog is dead

How will it be
to lie in the sky
without roof or door
and wind for an eye

With cloud for shift
how will I hide?

Mona Van Duyn

1921–

From *To See, To Take* by Mona
Van Duyn. Copyright © 1966,
1970 by Mona Van Duyn. Reprinted by permission of Athe-
neum Publishers. Appeared origi-
nally in *Quarterly Review of
Literature*.

Leda*

*"Did she put on his knowledge with his power
Before the indifferent beak could let her drop?"*

Not even for a moment. He knew, for one thing, what he was.
When he saw the swan in her eyes he could let her drop.
In the first look of love men find their great disguise,
and collecting these rare pictures of himself was his life.

Her body became the consequence of his juice,
while her mind closed on a bird and went to sleep.
Later, with the children in school, she opened her eyes
and saw her own openness, and felt relief.

In men's stories her life ended with his loss.

She stiffened under the storm of his wings to a glassy shape,
stricken and mysterious and immortal. But the fact is,
she was not, for such an ending, abstract enough.

She tried for a while to understand what it was
that had happened, and then decided to let it drop.
She married a smaller man with a beaky nose,
and melted away in the storm of everyday life.

*Composed in response to William Butler Yeats' Leda and the Swan.

Diane Wakoski
1937–

From *Discrepancies and Apparitions*, a volume of *Trilogy* by Diane Wakoski. Copyright © 1967 by Diane Wakoski. Reprinted by permission of Doubleday and Co., Inc.

Inside Out

I walk the purple carpet into your eye,
carrying the silver butter server,
but a truck rumbles by,
                leaving its black tire prints on my foot,
and old images—
        the sound of banging screen doors on hot afternoons
        and a fly buzzing over Kool-Aid spilled on the sink—
flicker, as reflections on the metal surface.

Come in, you said,
inside your paintings, inside the blood factory, inside the
old songs that line your hands, inside
eyes that change like a snowflake every second,

inside spinach leaves holding that one piece of gravel,

inside the whiskers of a cat,

inside your old hat, and most of all inside your mouth where you
grind the pigments with your teeth, painting
with a broken bottle on the floor, and painting
with an ostrich feather on the moon that rolls out of my mouth.

You cannot let me walk inside you too long
inside the veins where my small feet touch
bottom.
You must reach inside and pull me
like a silver bullet
from your arm.

A Chronology of Poetry

Babylonian *Epic of Gilgamesh*, one of the earliest major national poems, relates adventures of the legendary Sumerian king

c. 2000 B.C. Renaissance of Sumerian culture under Gudea; Babylonian mathematics reaches a high level of sophistication

An Ionian bard we know as Homer shapes the tales of the Trojan War into two massive folk epics, the *Iliad* and the *Odyssey*

c. 800-750 Greek monarchies are gradually replaced by aristocracies, former kings either exiled or reduced to titular offices

Philosophical meditations on farm labor and contemporary Greek society are the subject matter of Hesiod's *Works and Days*

c. 750-700 Greeks adapt Phoenician alphabet to their own language; Greek cultural renaissance

Birth of Archilochus, the skeptical Greek poet known for his bitterly antiheroic verses

714

Birth of Sappho, famed for her sentimental lyric poetry and later dubbed the "tenth muse" by Classical poets

612 Increased militarization of the Spartan state takes place after Second Messenian War

Birth of Pindar, creator of aristocratic odes celebrating victors of the Greek athletic games

518

509 Founding of the Roman Republic

Indian *Mahabharata*, perhaps the longest poem ever composed, recounts the internecine struggle between descendants of King Bharata; portions of the *Ramayana* are written

c. 500 Proscribed taboos mark the beginning of caste stratification in India

Aristotle writes the *Poetics*, a treatise on the origin and nature of poetry

335-22 Hellenism spreads through the conquests of Alexander the Great

Life of Lucretius, author of the Epicurian didactic poem *On the Nature of Things*

99-55 Period of internal strife and warring within Roman Empire culminates in the formation of Rome's First Triumvirate (60)

Birth of Catullus, first Roman poet to use classical lyric meters

87 Civil war rages in Rome; Sulla conquers the city, effects temporary conservative reforms

Vergil begins the *Georgics*, a four-book poem devoted to the subject of agriculture, and completes the ten bucolic *Eclogues*

37 Second Roman Triumvirate—Antony, Lepidus, and Octavian—is renewed for five more years

Death of Vergil; his *Aeneid*, modeled on Homer's epics, is greeted with enthusiasm in Rome

19 Rule of Augustus over Roman Empire well established; emperor institutes beneficial reforms

Death of the Roman master of elegy, Propertius; two years later Horace writes *Ars Poetica*, proposing guidelines for writing poetry

13 Following death of Roman chief priest Lepidus, Augustus attempts to revitalize state religion with exotic Eastern cult influences

4 Birth of Jesus of Nazareth

Ovid completes *Ars Amatoria*, a sophisticated compendium of love; shortly thereafter his *Metamorphosis* appears

3 Tiberius remains in Rhodes in retirement until the death of Augustus' successors compels him to return to Rome as only heir to the title

Augustus orders the destruction of Ovid's works and banishes the poet from Rome

A.D. 8

Silver Age of Roman literature flourishes with the poetry of Persius, Juvenal, Martial, Lucan, and Petronius, probable author of the *Satyricon*

14-192 Death of Augustus followed by successive reigns of Julio-Claudian, Flavian, and Antonine emperors

General decline of literary forms, including poetry, in Roman Empire; appearance of *Daphnis and Chloë*, attributed to Greek poet Longus

192-284 Death of last Antonine emperor, Commodus; complete political and economic collapse throughout the Mediterranean

Arya Sura versifies in the Indian *Jatakamala* tales of the former births of Buddha

477-495 Rule of Budhagupta, last emperor of Indian Gupta dynasty; golden age of classical Sanskrit

Byzantine poet Romanos creates the first religious poetry; Greek classical verse enjoys a renaissance

527-565 Reign of Byzantine emperor Justinian

639 Following reign of Dagobert, feudal decentralization replaces royal power in Frankish kingdom

787 First recorded raid of the Danes in England

800 Charlemagne crowned Holy Roman Emperor

Beowulf, the earliest surviving narrative poem in English, is written

The *chanson de geste* replaces the epic as the preferred form for heroic verse narrative

1100-1200 Revival of town life in Western Europe, notably in communes and peasant associations of France

Icelandic poets assemble fragmentary traditional verses to compile the *Poetic Edda*

1100 Henry I succeeds the hated William II in England; promises reform with the *Coronation Charter*

	Year	
An anonymous German poet bases *The Nibelungenlied* on German and Scandinavian legends	1200	German civil war rages; rival kings Philip of Swabia and Otto of Brunswick vie for crown
Guillaume de Lorris writes the first part of *Romance of the Rose*, an allegory completed by Jean de Meung some forty-five years later	1230	Campaign of Henry III in France; Ferdinand III unites Léon to Castile
The Mabinogion, a versified collection of Welsh tales about the legendary King Arthur, is committed to writing for the first time	1300-1425	
Dante Alighieri completes *The Divine Comedy*, a philosophical-political epic based on the theology and cosmology of St. Thomas of Aquinas	1321	
	1338	Outbreak of the Hundred Years' War
An unknown poet creates *Sir Gawain and the Green Knight*, a landmark of English literature	1370	Black Prince sacks Limoges; French defeat English in Gascony and Maine
Strongly influenced by Boccaccio's *Il Filostrata*, Geoffrey Chaucer sets down the humorous verses of *Troilus and Criseyde*	1385	Anglo-French war renewed after a six-year truce; Richard II's attempt to set up a personal government is blocked by Parliament
Allegorical satire *Piers Plowman* is written, reputedly by poet William Langland	1387	Lords appellant, led by the duke of Gloucester, seek to impeach members of Richard's party
Chaucer finishes his longest and finest work, the bawdy *Canterbury Tales*	1400	Henry IV suppresses rebellions organized on behalf of the deposed Richard; Richard dies in Tower
François Villon murders a thief during a street brawl; thereafter he repeatedly involves himself in illegal escapades for which he is arrested, jailed, and ultimately sentenced to exile	1455	Conflict between houses of York and Lancaster erupts in Wars of the Roses; Richard, Duke of York, reinstated as protector, only to be removed again the following year
Villon reviews his rogue's life in the bitter yet pathetic ballads of the *Grand Testament*	1461	Defeated at Towton, Henry VI flees to Scotland; Edward IV crowned
Advent of printing dramatically increases the availability of poetry to the general public	1476	William Caxton establishes his printing press at Westminster
Romantic epic becomes popular in Italy; Ludovico Ariosto writes *Orlando furioso*	1532	Refusing to validate Henry VIII's Act of Supremacy over the Church, Thomas More resigns as Lord Chancellor and is subsequently executed
Joachim DuBellay publishes *Défense et Illustration de la Langue française*; the treatise sets forth tenets of the Pléiade, whose members produce the true French Renaissance poetic form	1549	England declares war on France; Protestant doctrines introduced in England
After seventeen years of work, Luís Vaz de Camões completes his epic *Lusiads*, a celebration of Portugal's international destiny	1572	St. Bartholomew's Day Massacre of French Protestants at Paris; Sir Francis Drake attacks Spanish harbors in America
Pierre Ronsard publishes his last and best collection of love poetry, *Sonnets pour Hélène*	1578	James VI takes over the Scottish government; Wilna and Altdorf universities founded
Torquato Tasso's *Gerusalemme liberata* published	1581	James VI signs second Scottish Confession of Faith
Sir Philip Sidney's *Astrophel and Stella* establishes the sonnet sequence in England	1584	Parliament passes bill prohibiting plots against the queen; Elizabeth expels Jesuits and priests
Edmund Spenser introduces the Spenserian stanza in the first three books of his romantic tribute to Queen Elizabeth, *The Faerie Queen*	1590	Henry IV defeats the League of Sixteen in the Battle of Ivry
William Shakespeare's first published poem, *Venus and Adonis*, appears; one year later *The Rape of Lucrece* is printed	1593	Henry IV abjures the reformed religion at St. Denis, adopts Catholicism, and is crowned at Chartres the following year
Spenser composes *Astrophel* in honor of Sir Philip Sidney and completes the autobiographical bucolic poem *Colin Clout Comes Home Againe*	1595	
Shakespeare finishes *Julius Caesar*	1600	East India Company is established
Christopher Marlowe writes *Dr. Faustus*, a drama in blank verse	1604	James I declares peace with Spain; Robert Catesby instigates Gunpowder Plot
Shakespeare completes two of his greatest tragedies, *King Lear* and *Macbeth*; three years later his *Sonnets* are published	1606	Parliament passes penal laws against papists; plague in London kills thousands
Death of Shakespeare in Stratford, three years after completing his last work, *Henry VIII*	1616	Cardinal Richelieu becomes French Secretary of State under Louis XIII
Academie française is founded to carry on the work of the Pléiade	1630	Treaty of Madrid ends war between England and Spain
While a student at Cambridge, John Milton writes his companion poems *L'Allegro* and *Il Penseroso;* two years later he creates the masque *Comus*	1632	Richelieu suppresses insurrection headed by Gaston of Orleans, heir presumptive to the throne, and the duke of Montmorency
Collected works of metaphysical poet John Donne are published posthumously; George Herbert, Donne's most representative successor, dies	1633	Galileo Galilei is forced by the Inquisition to abjure the theories of Copernicus

Milton travels to Italy to continue his studies and while there writes the elegy *Lycidas*	1638	Emergence of Scottish Covenanters with signing of Solemn League and Covenant
Milton's renowned national epic *Paradise Lost* is published, followed four years later by a sequel, *Paradise Regained*; John Dryden is named Poet Laureate in England after the appearance of his poem on the Dutch War, *Annus Mirabilis*	1667	Treaties of Breda end war between England and Holland; emergence of court and country factions foreshadows the later Tory and Whig parties in England
Dryden satirizes contemporary political figures in *Absalom and Achitophel*	1682	Radical members of Shaftsbury's country faction plot against policies of Charles II
Matthew Prior and Charles Montagu parody Dryden's *The Hind and the Panther* in *The City Mouse and the Country Mouse*	1687	James II grants freedom of worship to all denominations in the first Declaration of Liberty of Conscience
Dryden's eloquent Pindaric ode *Alexander's Feast* is followed, two years later, with *Fables, Ancient and Modern*, his last great work	1697	Treaty of Ryswick between France, England, Spain, and Holland acknowledges William III as king of England and Anne as his heir presumptive
Alexander Pope's *An Essay on Criticism* draws heavily on Horace's *Ars Poetica*	1711	Joseph Addison and Richard Steele begin publishing *The Spectator* in England
John Gay writes the satirical eclogues *Shepherd's Week*; the following year Prior composes *Alma*	1714	Peace of Utrecht signed between Spain and Holland; George I succeeds Queen Anne
Gay writes his best-known work, *The Beggar's Opera*, and its widely read sequel, *Polly*	1728	First Parliament of George II; Prado convention ends war between England and Spain
Pope expresses his deistic philosophy in *An Essay on Man*	1734	Opening of London's Royal Opera House, Covent Garden; J.S. Bach composes *Christmas Oratorio*
Thomas Gray treats man's tragic dignity in *Elegy Written in a Country Churchyard*	1751	England finally accedes to the Austro-Russian alliance made in 1746
Oliver Goldsmith enters the literary limelight with his didactic poem *The Traveller*	1765	Parliament issues Stamp Act, first direct tax levied by Crown on American colonies
Romantic writings of Rousseau inspire the formation of *Sturm und Drang*, the literary movement leading to German Romanticism	1770	French dauphin marries Marie Antoinette; colonists killed in Boston Massacre; Townshend Acts repealed except for tea tax
Samuel Johnson compiles a series of biographical and critical essays in *Lives of the Poets*	1781	Rousseau writes his *Confessions;* Kant, *A Critique of Pure Reason*
Mystic and visionary poet William Blake's *Poetical Sketches* contains his earliest verses	1783	Treaty of Paris is signed between England, France, Spain, Holland, and U.S.; England recognizes U.S. independence
Works of Friedrich von Schiller, Novalis, and Johann Wolfgang von Goethe usher in the Romantic era in Germany	1788	United States Constitution is ratified; New York declared Federal capital and seat of Congress
Blake engraves and publishes *Songs of Innocence*	1789	Parisians storm the Bastille; Declaration of Rights of Man published
After a year abroad, William Wordsworth returns to England imbued with the republican spirit of the French revolutionaries; shortly thereafter he begins his long friendship with Samuel Coleridge	1792	French mobs storm Tuileries; Swiss Guard massacred and royal family imprisoned in Temple; French Republic proclaimed; trial of Louis XIV begins; king found guilty and sentenced to death
Coleridge publishes his first volume of verse, *Poems on Various Occasions*	1796	Bonaparte defeats Austrians at Lodi and Arcola; John Adams elected second president of U.S.
Coleridge and Wordsworth collaborate on *Lyrical Ballads*, a manifesto for Romantic poets; Coleridge contributes the *Rime of the Ancient Mariner* and completes *Cristobel, Part 1* and *Kubla Khan*	1798	Malthus writes an *Essay on the Principle of Population;* Edward Jenner discovers a vaccine for smallpox; Aloys Senefelder invents lithography
Blake completes his metaphysical *Prophetic Books* and *Milton;* begins *Jerusalem*	1804	Bonaparte crowned emperor as Napoleon I
Wordsworth dedicates his autobiographical poem *The Prelude* to Coleridge	1805	Great Britain joins with Austria, Russia, and Sweden in Third Coalition against France
Goethe presents the Faust legend in his verse-drama of the same name	1808	French invade Spain; Charles IV and son Ferdinand renounce Spanish throne in favor of Napoleon's brother Joseph Bonaparte
Shelley expelled from Oxford for the publication of *The Necessity of Atheism*	1811	Birth of an heir to Napoleon and Archduchess Marie Louise, daughter of Francis I of Austria
Byron's tour of Europe inspires the first two cantos of *Childe Harold's Pilgrimage*	1812	America declares war on England; Napoleon invades Russia, is repelled at Beresina
Byron marries Isabella Milbanke; leaving her the following year, he travels with Shelley in Switzerland, where *The Prisoner of Chillon* and two more cantos of *Childe Harold* are written	1815	Holy Alliance formed by Russia, Austria, and Prussia; Wellington and Blücher defeat Napoleon at Waterloo; second Peace of Paris is signed
Addicted to laudanum and estranged from his family, Coleridge settles in Highgate in search of a cure; Shelley marries Mary Godwin after his desertion precipitates his first wife's suicide; leaves England permanently two years later	1816	First protective tariff enacted in U.S.; Elgin Marbles bought by the British Museum; Karl August of Saxe-Weimar grants first German constitution

Keats publishes his first volume of poems; Byron creates the "Byronic hero" in the Faustian verse-drama *Manfred*; it is followed shortly by *Beppo* and *The Vision of Judgment*	1817
Keats composes *Endymion*, begins *La Belle Dame Sans Merci* and *The Eve of St. Agnes*	1818
Keats's *Ode to a Nightingale, Ode to a Grecian Urn*, and *To Autumn* appear in print; works of Victor Hugo, Lamartine, Musset, Vigny herald the Romantic movement in France; Shelley finishes *Prometheus Unbound*	1820
Keats dies of tuberculosis at age twenty-six; after writing *Adonais* in memory of Keats, Shelley drowns while sailing off the Italian coast	1821
Byron joins Greek insurgent forces, dies of malaria; his satirical *Don Juan* left unfinished	1824
Hugo composes *Les Orientales*; the following year Alfred Tennyson writes *Timbuctoo*	1828
Hugo completes the richly romantic *Les Feuilles d'Automne*; Aleksandr Pushkin models *Eugene Onegin* on Byron's *Don Juan*	1831
Goethe's *Faust, Part II* is published posthumously; Tennyson's collected *Poems* are printed; Robert Browning's first published work, *Pauline*, is greeted with supreme indifference	1832
Philologist Elias Lönnrott compiles the Finnish national epic, the *Kalevala*	1835
	1837
Browning writes the poignant *Pippa Passes*	1841
Tennyson expresses growing misgivings about the scientific age in his second collection of poems, which includes *Ulysses* and *Morte d'Arthur*	1842
Browning secretly marries Elizabeth Barrett; he finds his ideal medium in the poems of *Bells and Pomegrantes*	1846
Tennyson is named Poet Laureate in response to *In Memoriam*; Browning completes *Christmas Eve, Easter Day*; Elizabeth Barrett Browning, *Sonnets from the Portuguese*	1850
Walt Whitman publishes, at his own expense, the strikingly original collection of poems *Leaves of Grass*; Browning writes *Men and Women*	1855
Charles Baudelaire's notorious symbolist work *Les Fleurs du Mal* is condemned as obscene	1857
Emily Dirkinson begins writing poetry; of nearly 1,800 poems amassed, only seven are published during her lifetime	1860
Algernon Swinburne wins fame with *Atalanta in Calydon*; the following year his *Poems and Ballads* is attacked for its anti-Victorian sentiments; Whitman versifies his impression of the Civil War in *Drum Taps;* William Butler Yeats is born	1865
John Greenleaf Whittier, famed for his evocative poems of rural New England, recalls his Massachusetts boyhood in *Snow-Bound*	1866
Browning finishes the fourth and last volume of his versified murder story *The Ring and the Book*	1869
Arthur Rimbaud creates some of the earliest surrealist poetic images in *Le Bateau Ivre*; two years later *Une Saison en Enfer* appears	1871
Erstwhile Parnassian and Décadent poet Paul Verlaine deserts his wife for a vagabond liaison with the erratic Rimbaud; his *Romance sans paroles* is inspired by the duo's travels	1872
Stephane Mallarmé produces *L'Apres-midi d'un faune*, the eclogue that inspires Debussy's tone-poem; Lewis Carroll writes *The Hunting of the Snark*, a nonsense fantasy	1876
The Browning Society is formed	1881

Right column details:

1817 — Anglo-Spanish treaty opens West Indian trade to U.K.; David Ricardo writes *Principles of Political Economy and Taxation*; first exhibition of John Constable's landscapes

1818 — First steamer, the *Savannah*, crosses the Atlantic in twenty-six days

1820 — Missouri Compromise prohibits slavery in Louisiana Territory north of Missouri's southern border; England's George III succeeded by George IV; Malthus writes *Principles of Political Economy*

1821 — Death of Napoleon on St. Helena; Sir Walter Scott writes *Kenilworth*; Mexico wins its independence from Spain

1824 — First trade union is formed in England; Charles X subdues growing liberalism in France

1828 — Andrew Jackson elected President; he introduces the spoils system on a national level

1831 — Nat Turner leads major slave revolt in Virginia; William Lloyd Garrison founds *The Liberator*, an antislavery journal

1832 — Construction of London's National Gallery begins; French take Antwerp, forcing Holland to recognize Belgium; Irish Reform Bill passed

1835 — First German railway connects Nürnberg and Fürth; Texas declares independence from Mexico

1837 — Beginning of Queen Victoria's sixty-four year reign

1841 — First issue of *Punch* magazine published

1842 — Dickens' maiden tour of the U.S.; Honoré de Balzac issues first volume of *La Comédie humaine*; Chartists riot in England

1846 — Beginning of war between United States and Mexico over Texas and other western territories

1850 — American Compromise of 1850 attempts to balance slavery and antislavery interests

1855 — Paris International Exposition testifies to technological and economic progress of France; Piedmont joins in Crimean War

1857 — Irish Republican Brotherhood founded; Anglo-French seizure of Canton in T'ai P'ing Rebellion

1860 — Abraham Lincoln elected President of U.S.; North Carolina secedes from union; French and English occupy Peking

1865 — Lincoln assassinated; the Thirteenth Amendment, abolishing slavery, ratified; Lee surrenders at Appomattox Courthouse ending American Civil War; Joseph Lister introduces surgical asepsis

1866 — Prussians emerge victorious in Seven Week' War against Austria; humiliated French concede to North German Confederation the next year

1869 — Fifteenth Amendment, giving blacks the right to vote, is proposed by Congress and ratified the following year

1871 — German Empire is proclaimed; Heinrich Schleimann identifies and excavates site of ancient Troy; trade unions legalized in England

1872 — Ballot Act legalizes secret voting in England; George Eliot completes *Middlemarch*; dance impresario Sergei Diaghilev is born

1876 — General Custer and troops massacred by Sitting Bull's Sioux Indians at Little Bighorn; Alexander Graham Bell invents the telephone; Queen Victoria declared Empress of India

1881 — Ferdinand De Lesseps begins Panama Canal

Death of Henry Wadsworth Longfellow, author of the memorable *Children's Hour, Hiawatha, Wreck of the Hesperus,* and *The Village Blacksmith*	1882	Britain occupies Egypt; beginning of German colonialism marked by increased tension between that country and Britain
Tennyson completes last volume of *Idylls of the King;* Jules La Forgue's *Les Complaintes* is one of the earliest poems composed in *vers libre*	1885	Fabian Society founded; Irish land bill, the Ashbourne Act, provides funds for Irish tenants to purchase their holdings
William Butler Yeats' intense nationalism reveals itself in *The Wanderings of Oisin*	1889	Trade unionism spreads to unskilled workers in great London dock strike
Mabel Todd and T.W. Higginson begin the posthumous publication of Emily Dickinson's poems	1890	First international congress for protection of workers convenes in Berlin
Yeats helps found the Irish Literary Theatre, later named the Abbey Theatre; abandoning the novel, Thomas Hardy turns to poetry; writes *Wessex Poems,* first of six volumes of lyric verse	1898	Curies discover radium; Zeppelin invents his airship; Spanish-American War breaks out after battleship *Maine* is blown up in Havana harbor; Spain grants Cuba independence
With *In the Seven Woods* Yeats moves toward satire and realism; seven years later he finishes *The Green Helmet and Other Poems*	1903	Orville and Wilbur Wright fly their first airplane at Kitty Hawk, N.C.; Russian Labor Party splits into Mensheviks and Bolsheviks
Rainer Maria Rilke expands the new poetic form, the *Dinggedicht,* in a collection entitled *Neue Gedichte*	1907	Second Hague Peace Conference held; Japanese immigration to U.S. restricted; Lumière invents color photography
Ezra Pound, chief promulgator of poetic "imagism," publishes his first poems under the title *A Lume Spento;* Hardy versifies the Napoleonic wars in *The Dynasts*	1908	German Social Democrats rally at Nürnberg; Revisionists defeat Marxists; Austria annexes Bosnia and Herzegovina; works of Kandinsky mark beginning of abstract art
Refused publication in the U.S., Robert Frost establishes his reputation in England with *A Boy's Will* and *North of Boston*	1912	War in the Balkans; Chinese republic is proclaimed; Casimir Funk discovers vitamins
	1914	Outbreak of World War I
Thomas Stearns Eliot settles in London, where he falls under the influence of Pound	1915	German submarine sinks the *Lusitania;* Germany and Britain declare mutual blockade
Yeats marries spiritual medium Georgie Hyde Lees, who inspires such poems as *The Wild Swans at Coole* and *Four Plays for Dancers*	1917	U.S. breaks off diplomatic relations with Germany; Congress declares war on Germany and passes Selective Service Act
T.S. Eliot publishes *The Waste Land;* his revolutionary approach to poetic expression establishes him as avant-garde leader in the field; Yeats elected senator of Irish Free State; John Crowe Ransom helps found The Fugitives, a Nashville literary group	1922	Reparation Commission declares "deliberate default" by Germany; U.S., Britain, and Japan agree to limit naval forces at Washington Arms Conference; Irish Free State is established
Frost writes his prize-winning *New Hampshire;* Wallace Stevens searches for the order in chaos in his first volume of poems, *Harmonium;* Rilke probes Existentialism in the *Duino Elegies;* E. E. Cummings affects eccentric punctuation, typography, and language in *Tulips and Chimneys*	1923	Hitler's "beer hall putsch" quelled in Munich; U.S. recalls occupation forces from Rhineland; Reparations Commission appoints committee to examine German economic conditions
Ransom mocks the courtly, elegant world of the southern aristocrat in *Chills and Fever*	1924	Lenin dies; Joseph Stalin becomes ultimate dictator in Russia
Pound publishes *Cantos I-XVI*	1925	Death of Sun Yat-sen, father of Chinese republic
D.H. Lawrence's iconoclastic collection *Pansies* is censored by British authorities	1929	Stock market crash on Wall Street leads to worldwide economic depression
Eliot celebrates the joys of Christianity in the poetic liturgy *Ash Wednesday*	1930	Mahatma Gandhi initiates civil disobedience campaign in India
The Collected Poems of Yeats, containing some of the poet's best works, includes *Leda and the Swan* and *Sailing to Byzantium*	1933	Adolf Hitler becomes chancellor of Germany; suppresses German trade unions and forbids formation of political parties other than Nazi
Dylan Thomas publishes his controversial collection *Eighteen Poems*	1934	German-Polish ten-year nonagression pact signed; Germany suspends all debt payments abroad
T.S. Eliot writes *Murder in the Cathedral,* a play in blank verse; completing *Ideas of Order,* Stevens begins *The Man with the Blue Guitar*	1935	Germany repudiates military clauses of Versailles treaty; President Roosevelt signs Social Security Act in U.S.
Frost writes *A Further Range*	1936	Germany occupies demilitarized Rhineland zone
W.H. Auden's change in views from socialism to Christianity is the subject of *New Year Letter*	1941	Japanese attack Pearl Harbor; the United States enters World War II
Frost's *A Witness Tree* wins for the poet his fourth Pulitzer Prize; Eliot completes *Four Quartets,* a series of meditative poems	1943	German defeat at Stalingrad marks turning point in war on eastern front; Italy surrenders to Allies and declares war on Germany
Robert Lowell, originator of the "confessional" style, rebels against the corruption of the times in his first collection, *Land of Unlikeness*	1944	Allied landing in Normandy; Moscow conference between Churchill and Stalin

Auden completes *For the Time Being* and *A Christmas Oratorio*; Pound, arrested for broadcasting Fascist propaganda to the U.S., writes the *Pisan Cantos* while in prison	1945
Pound, tried and found insane, is committed to a mental hospital for twelve years	1946
Auden composes *Age of Anxiety*; Lowell's *Lord Weary's Castle* wins the Pulitzer Prize	1947
Allen Ginsberg experiences his first mystical visions while reading Blake's poems; Eliot wins the Nobel Prize for Literature	1948
Sylvia Plath attempts suicide after a whirlwind summer internship at *Mademoiselle* in New York	1953
Dylan Thomas's *Under Milk Wood* is published posthumously; Theodore Roethke wins Pulitzer Prize for his *Collected Poems*	1954
Stevens's *Collected Poems* wins Pulitzer Prize	1955
Ginsberg scandalizes complacent America with publication of *Howl*; Plath marries British poet Ted Hughes; after a nervous breakdown, Anne Sexton begins writing poetry as therapy	1956
William Carlos Williams completes *Paterson*; Roethke awarded Bollinger Prize for *Words of the Winds*; Cummings's *95 Poems* published	1958
Writing in Lowell's "confessional" style, Sexton pours out the agony of her existence in *To Bedlam and Part Way Back*; Lowell wins National Book Award for his *Life Studies*	1960
Roethke composes the lighthearted *I Am! Says the Lamb*; Ginsberg's *Kaddish* and *Empty Mirror: Early Poems* are published	1961
First English translation of Yevgeny Yevtushenko's *Selected Poems* contains the controversial protest against anti-Semitism, *Babi Yar*; Iosef Brodsky writes his early poems in U.S.S.R.	1962
Plath commits suicide at age 31; her collections *Ariel* and *Crossing the Water* are published posthumously; Yevtushenko writes *A Precious Biography*; Brodsky, the *Elegy for John Donne*	1963
Accused of "social parasitism," Brodsky is sentenced to five years forced labor in a Soviet work camp; Imamu Amiri Baraka, (LeRoi Jones) writes *The Dutchman* and *The Toilet*	1964
John Berryman's acrid *77 Dream Songs* wins the Pulitzer Prize	1965
Ginsberg arrested and charged with obscenity during a poetry reading at the Spoleto Festival; Sexton's despairing *Live or Die* wins Pulitzer Prize; Yevtushenko writes *Bratsk Station*	1967
Lowell's *Notebooks 1967–68* revitalizes poetry with its fresh treatment of the sonnet	1968
Berryman treats the theme of his father's suicide in *His Toy, His Dream, His Rest*	1969
Chilean poet and militant Communist Pablo Neruda is awarded the Nobel Prize for Literature	1971
Berryman leaps to his death from a bridge in Minneapolis; Sexton summons primal energies of children in *Transformations*; Brodsky, exiled from U.S.S.R., accepts lecturer's post at University of Michigan; Pound dies in Venice	1972
Ginsberg's *The Fall of America* considers the state of America and the state of his life; Lowell publishes *History, For Lizzie and Harriet*, and the Pulitzer Prize-winning *Dolphin*	1973
Sexton commits suicide	1974
Sexton's last volume of poetry, *The Awful Rowing Toward God*, is a comment on the self-destructive impulses of the modern generation	1975

1945	Allies defeat German forces; first atomic bombs dropped on Hiroshima and Nagasaki to end war in Pacific; United Nations organized
1946	Winston Churchill's "Iron Curtain" speech notes beginning of Cold War
1947	George C. Marshall proposes plan for European recovery; Truman Doctrine implemented
1948	Assassination of Mahatma Gandhi; state of Israel is created; Alger Hiss convicted of perjury
1953	Joseph Stalin dies; Korean armistice is signed
1954	U.S. Supreme Court outlaws racial segregation in public schools; formation of SEATO and beginning of U.S. financial aid to Indochina
1955	Martin Luther King leads bus boycott in Alabama
1956	Suez Canal crisis; U.S.S.R. crushes anti-Communist uprising in Hungary
1958	National Aeronautics and Space Administration created to study problems of space travel
1960	American U-2 reconaissance plane, shot down over Soviet territory, creates tension between the two countries; Organization for Economic Cooperation and Development set up
1961	Berlin Wall built; Soviet's Yuri Gagarin becomes first man in space; World Food Program for relief of hunger and famine established
1962	U Thant elected secretary general of U.N.; John Glenn becomes first American to orbit earth; seventeen-nation Disarmament Conference is held in Geneva
1963	President John F. Kennedy assassinated; United States, Soviet Union, and Britain sign limited test ban treaty in Moscow; Martin Luther King leads "March on Washington"
1964	U.S. Congress passes Civil Rights Act; race riots erupt in many northern cities; Johnson Administration creates Office of Economic Opportunity to help fight poverty
1965	U.S. begins bombing North Vietnam; Mao Tse-tung launches "cultural revolution" in China
1967	Arab-Israeli Six-Day War breaks out; Dr. Christiaan Barnard performs the first heart transplant; crisis in Cyprus; U.N. assembly adopts declaration eliminating discrimination against women
1968	Russian troops invade Czechoslovakia to stifle liberal regime of Alexander Dubcek
1969	American astronauts Armstrong and Aldrin become first men to walk on the moon
1971	U.S. Congress passes Constitutional amendment lowering the voting age to eighteen
1972	President Richard Nixon visits Peking in a "journey for peace"; Britain imposes direct rule over Northern Ireland after fifty-one years of semi-autonomous rule by that country
1973	Yom Kippur War breaks out between Israel and Arab states; oil price increases lead to world economic crisis; agreement is signed to end Vietnam War
1974	President Nixon, facing impeachment over Watergate scandal, resigns
1975	Britain votes to stay in Common Market; South Vietnam and Cambodia fall to Communists; first joint U.S.–Soviet space mission succeeds

Selected Bibliography

Auden, W. H. *The Dyer's Hand and Other Essays*. New York: Random House, 1962.

Bodkin, Maud. *Archetypal Patterns in Poetry*. London: Oxford University Press, 1963.

Brereton, Geoffrey. *An Introduction to the French Poets: Villon to the Present Day*. London: Methuen, 1956.

Brooks, Cleanth. *Modern Poetry and the Tradition*. Chapel Hill: University of North Carolina Press, 1967.

Eliot, T. S. *The Sacred Wood: Essays on Poetry and Criticism*. London: Methuen, 1932.

Encyclopedia of Poetry and Poetics. Alex Preminger, ed. Princeton: Princeton University Press, 1974.

Finley, M. I. *The World of Odysseus*. New York: Meridian Books, 1959.

Hazlitt, William. "Lectures on the English Poets," *Complete Works*. P. P. Howe, ed. Vol. 5. London: J. M. Dent, 1930–34.

Highet, Gilbert. *Poets in a Landscape*. New York: Knopf, 1957.

Jaeger, Werner. *Paideia: The Ideals of Greek Culture*. 3 vols. New York: Oxford University Press, 1945.

Johnson, Samuel. *Lives of the English Poets*. G. B. Hill, ed. New York: Octagon Books, 1967.

Keats, John. *The Letters of John Keats*. 2 vols. Hyder Rollins, ed. Cambridge: Harvard University Press, 1958.

Lowenfels, Walter, ed. *In A Time of Revolution: Poems from Our Third World*. New York: Random House, 1969.

Marks, Emerson R. *The Poetics of Reason*. New York: Random House, 1968.

Neff, Edward E. *A Revolution in European Poetry, 1660–1900*. New York: Columbia University Press, 1940.

Peacock, Thomas L. *The Four Ages of Poetry*. Bound with *A Defence of Poetry* by Shelley, Percy B., John E. Jordan, ed. New York: Bobbs-Merrill, 1965.

The Poem Itself: 45 Modern Poets in a New Presentation. Stanley Burnshaw, ed. New York: Holt, Rinehart, and Winston, 1960.

Richards, I. A. *Practical Criticism: A Study of Literary Judgment*. London: Kegan Paul, 1929.

Skelton, Robin. *Cavalier Poets*. London: Longmans, Green, 1960.

Stevens, Wallace. *The Necessary Angel*. New York: Knopf, 1951.

Picture Credits

The Editors would like to thank Russell Ash in London, Barbara Nagelsmith in Paris, and Lynn Seiffer in New York for their invaluable assistance.

The following abbreviations are used:

BN	—Bibliothèque Nationale, Paris	(MA)	—Mondadori Archives
BM	—British Museum	NPG	—National Portrait Gallery, London
(WC)	—Woodfin Camp Associates		
CP	—Culver Pictures, New York	NYPL	—New York Public Library
GC	—The Granger Collection, New York	PML	—Pierpont Morgan Library
		(RM)	—Rollie McKenna
MMA	—Metropolitan Museum of Art	(WW)	—Wide World Photos

HALF-TITLE: Symbol designed by Jay J. Smith Studio FRONTISPIECE: (Patrick Ward—WC)

CHAPTER 1 **6** Museum of Fine Arts, Boston, Goloubew Collection **8** Painting by Shokado Shojo, Edo period. Cleveland Museum of Art, Kern Collection **8–9** Spencer Collection, NYPL **11** *Thirty-six Immortal Poets*, by Tatebayashi Kagei, 18th c. Cleveland Museum of Art, Marlatt Fund **12** *Poppies and Quail* by Ando Hiroshige, 1835. MMA, Rogers Fund, 1918 **14–15** Both: *Alice's Adventures . . .* by Charles Dodgson. Rare Book Division, NYPL **16–17** *Krishna Overcoming the Naga Demon*, 18th c. MMA, Rogers Fund, 1927 **18** MMA, Rogers Fund, 1931

19 Carved scenes from life of Sigurd, Church of Hylestad, Norway. Universitetets Oldsaksamling, Oslo **20** and **21** Both: Scenes from King Arthur's life. Left: BN, Ms.Fr. 95 fol. 173v. Right: BN, Ms.Fr. 95 fol. 159v. **22** Left, BM MS. Cott. Vit.A. xv.f.132; Right, *Lemminkainen* by C.J. Sjostrand, 1872. Art Museum of the Ateneum, Helsinki **23** *Chronicle of the Cid*, Fadrique Aleman de Basilea, Burgos, 1512. Hispanic Society of America, New York **24** (MA) **24–25** First edition of *Orlando furioso* by Ludovico Ariosto, 1516. (MA) **25** Left, NYPL; Right, Title page of *Obras de Luis de Camões*, 1782. NYPL **26** (MA) **27** *Torquato Tasso* by Alessandro Allori. Uffizi Gallery, Florence (Scala) **28** Battle of Roncevalles from the *Song of Roland*. BN, Ms.Fr. 20128 f.233v. **29** Maugis taking Roland's swords from The *Song of Roland*. BN, Ms.Fr.5893 f.51v

CHAPTER 2 **30** Achilles, red-figured amphora, c.450–440 B.C. Vatican Museum (Hirmer) **32–33** Hoplites, Oinochoe Chigi Vase, c.650–640 B.C. Villa Giulia, Rome (Pucciarelli) **33** Black-figured amphora by Exekias. Vatican Museum (Scala) **35** *Apotheosis. . .*, 3rd c. B.C. BM **36** Attic vase, c.490–480 B.C. BM (Michael Holford) **37** Top, Terra-cotta vase, Rhodes, 600–575 B.C. MMA, Rogers Fund, 1956; Bottom, Calyx krater, mid-5th c. B.C. Cincinnati Art Museum, Semple Collection **38** Black-figured kylix, Athens, 6th c. B.C. MMA, Fletcher Fund, 1925 **39** Top, Bronze helmet fitting, 4th c. B.C. Staatliche Museum, Berlin; Bottom, Villa Albani, Rome **40** Cameo, 1st c. B.C. BM **41** *Georgics* by Vergil, 6th c. A.D. Vatican Library, Cod.Vat.Lat.3867 **42** Vergil mosaic. Bardo Museum, Tunis (Faillet-Ziolo) **43** Fresco of Aeneus, Pompeii. Museo Nazionale, Naples (Scala) **44** and **45** The *Aeneid* by Vergil. Vatican Library, Cod.Vat.Lat.3867 fols. 77 and 106 **46** *Ode II,20* by Horace. 10th c. A.D. BN Ms.Lat.7974 fol. 32 **47** Top, *Ovid* by Luca Signorelli. Duomo Orvieto (Scala) Bottom, Ovid's *Metamorphoses*, 1655. Bettmann Archive

CHAPTER 3 **48** *Troilus and Criseyde*, 1400. Corpus Christi College, Cambridge **50–51** Fresco of Dante, 1465. Florence Cathedral (Scala) **52–53** All: *The Divine Comedy*. Bibliotheca Laurenziana (MA) **54** *The Divine Comedy*. BN Ms. Ital. Cod.74 fol. lv **55** Title page of Dante's collected works, 16th c. Bibliotheca Trivulziana (MA) **56** *Tristan and Isolde*. BN Fr.103, f.1 **57** Top, *Canterbury Tales*, Ellesmere Ms. c. 1410. Facsimile edition Rare Book Division, NYPL, Original edition Huntington Library, San Marino; Bottom, *Romance of the Rose*. BN Ms. Fr.380 f.13v **58** *Canterbury Tales*, 14th c. British Library Manuscripts, Lansdowne 851 f.2 **59** Canterbury pilgrims. BM Ms. Royal 18 D.II f.148 (Michael Holford) **60–61** All: *Canterbury Tales*, Ellesmere manuscript, 1410. Facsimile edition Rare Book Division, NYPL **61** *Wynkyn de Worde*, 1497. The London Museum **62** *Piers Plowman*, 15th c. Huntington Library, San Marino **63** Gawain with his shield. 14th-15th c. PML Ms. 805 fol.48 **64** Both: *Gawain and the Green Knight*. British Library Manuscripts Ms. Cot.Nero AX Fol.94 V **65** *Les Ballades des pendus* by Villon, Paris 1489. BN

CHAPTER 4 **66** (Adam Woolfitt–WC)ᶠ **68** Top, Engraving of a printing shop, 16th c. Victoria and Albert Museum (John Webb); Bottom, Pierre de Ronsard. BN **69** Left, *Arcadia* by Sir Philip Sidney, 1598. BM (MA); Right, *The Faerie Queene* by Sir Edmund Spenser, 1590 Berg Collection, NYPL **70** Sir William Teshe's *A Booke containing . . . Hands . . .* , 1580. BM, Sloane Ms. 1832 f.7V **71** John Shakespeare's coat of arms, 1576. Shakespeare's Birthplace (MA) **72** Shakespeare's *Plays*, 1623. Folger Shakespeare Library **73** Shakespeare's *Sonnets*, 1609. (MA) **74** Top, *Paradise Lost* by John Milton, 1667. BM; Bottom, NYPL **75** Left, *John Milton*, Anon., 1629. NPG; Right, *Paradise Lost*, n.d. PML **77** *Distressed Poet* by William Hogarth, 1736. Birmingham City Museum and Art Gallery **78** Top, *Alexander Pope* by M. Dahl, 1727. NPG **78** and **79** Both: *Rape of the Lock* by Alexander Pope, 1714. Berg Collection, NYPL **79** Top, *Essay on Man* by Pope, 1733. PML

CHAPTER 5 **80** Daily Telegraph (Ian Yeomans–WC) **82** Top, *John Dryden* by Geoffrey Kneller, NPG **82–83** Drawing by Goethe of San Pietro Valley, 1787. Goethe National Museum, Weimar (MA) **83** *Goethe . . .* by Johann Tischbein, 1787. Staedel Institut, Frankfurt (Blauel) **84** *Hermann und Dorothea* by Goethe. Goethe Museum, Dusseldorf (MA) **85** Top, *Faust*, after a drawing by Rembrandt,

1650. (MA); Bottom, Goethe and secretary. Goethe Museum, Dusseldorf (MA) **86** Left, *Werther* by Goethe, 1774. Goethe Museum (MA); Right, Watercolor of Werther's suicide by Goethe, Goethe Museum, Frankfurt (MA) **87** Top, *William Blake* by Thomas Phillips, 1807. NPG; Center, *Johann von Schiller* by Ludovika Simanowitz, 1794. GC; Bottom, *Heinrich Heine* by C. Jager. GC **88** Left, *The Tyger, Songs of Innocence . . .* by William Blake, 1794. MMA, Rogers Fund, 1917; Right, *Robert Burns*, Burns Cottage, Alloway. (Julian Calder—WC) **89** left, GC; Right, *Sir Walter Scott* by J. P. Knight, Berg Collection, NYPL **90–91** *Percy Bysshe Shelley* by Joseph Severn. Kears and Shelley Memorial House, Rome **92** *The Cremation of Shelly's Body* by L.E. Fournier, 1889. Walker Art Gallery, Liverpool **93** *George Gordon, Lord Byron* by Thomas Phillips, 1814. NPG **94** Top left, *Manfred* by Byron, n.d. PML; Top right, *Childe Harold* by Byron, 1818. BM (MA); Bottom, *Fashionables of 1816* by I. R. Cruikshank. BM (Freeman) **95** *Aleksandr Pushkin* by W. Tropinin. Bettmann Archive **96–97** Engraving of a breakfast party by Charles Mottram. Victoria and Albert Museum (John Webb) **97** Left, *Samuel Taylor Coleridge* by R. Vandyke, 1795. NPG; Right, Engraving by Gustave Doré from *The Rime of the Ancient Mariner*, 1877. NYPL **98** *William Wordsworth* by Benjamin Haydon, 1818. NPG **99** (Daily Telegraph—WC) **100** Left, *John Keats* by Joseph Severn, 1821. NPG; Right, *Endymion* by Keats, 1817. PML

CHAPTER 6 **102** *The Sonnet* by William Mulready, 1839. Victoria and Albert Museum (John Webb) **104** *Robert Browning* by M. Gordigiani, 1858. NPG **105** *Elizabeth Barrett Browning* by F. Talfourd, 1859. NPG **106** *Robert Browning Taking Tea . . .* from *The Poet's Corner* by Max Beerbohm, 1904. Prints Division, NYPL **108** Photograph of Alfred, Lord Tennyson by Julia Margaret Cameron. MMA, Harris Brisbane Dick Fund, 1941 **109** Engraving by Gustave Doré from *Idylls of the King*, 1859. NYPL **110** Left, photograph of Hugo by Carat, 1802. BN; Right, Hugo's *Les Feuilles d'Automne*, 1831, BN (Roger Viollet) **111** *Le Légende de Siècles* by Hugo, 1860. Musée Hugo (Bulloz) **113** Caricature of Swinburne by "Ape" (Carlo Pellegrini), 1874. GC **114** Top, *Un Coin de Table* by Fantin-Latour (Bulloz); Left, *Le Fantôme* by Charles Baudelaire, designed by Rassenface, 1899. BN; Right, *Charles Baudelaire* (MA) **115** *Baudelaire* by Gustave Courbet. Montpellier (Bulloz) **116** Top left, Edgar Allan Poe by Mathew Brady, c. 1848. PML; Top right, *Perched Upon the Bust of Pallas*, by Manet from Poe's *The Raven*. Museum of Fine Arts, Boston; Bottom, *Ulalume* by Poe, 1849. PML **118–119** *Le Salon de Victor Hugo.* (MA) **120** *Two Were Immortal Twice* by Emily Dickinson, n.d. PML **121** CP **122** Top left, Self-portrait by Henry Wadsworth Longfellow, 1829. GC; Top right, CP; Lower left, daguerreotype of H.W. Longfellow. GC; Bottom, Brown Brothers **123** Left, Rare Book Division, NYPL; Right, *Whitman Inciting . . .* from *The Poet's Corner* by Max Beerbohm, 1904. Rare Book Division, NYPL

CHAPTER 7 **124** MMA, Alfred Stieglitz Collection, 1949 **126** Top, Brown Brothers; Bottom, *D. H. Lawrence* by J. Juta, 1920. NPG **127** *Thomas Hardy* by W. Strang, 1893. NPG **128** *Yeats at Petipa's* by John Sloan, 1910. Corcoran Gallery of Art **129** Top, *William Butler Yeats* by John Yeats, 1900. National Gallery of Ireland; Bottom, *Mr. W. B. Yeats Presenting . . .* from *The Poet's Corner* by Max Beerbohm, 1904. Bettmann Archive **130** *Vanity Fair*, June 1920. NYPL **131** Left, *Maud Gonne* by Sarah Purser. GC; Bottom, Easter Rebellion, 1916. (WW) **132** (RM) **133** Top left, CP; Right, *Over the Top*. Imperial War Museum; Bottom, CP **134** (RM) **135** Left, *Once by the Pacific* by Robert Frost. University of Virginia Library; Right, (RM) **136** *T. S. Eliot* by Wyndham Lewis, 1938. Fogg Art Museum, Harvard University Portrait Collection **137** *T S. Eliot* by Ronald Searle. Courtesy *Punch* **138** Kraushaar Galleries **139** Top left, Edna St. Vincent Millay by Arnold Genthe. Museum of Modern Art; Top right, (Bernard Gotfryd); Lower right, *Hart Crane* by Walker Evans. Liveright Publishing Corporation; Bottom, CP **140** (WW) **141** (RM)

CHAPTER 8 **142–145** All: (WW) **146** (WW) **146–147** (Layle Silbert **148** Top, (RM); Bottom, (Fay Godwin) **149** (Frank Murphy) **150** Both: (RM) **151** Top (RM); Bottom, Nancy Crampton **152** Victoria and Albert Museum (R. Todd-White)

Index